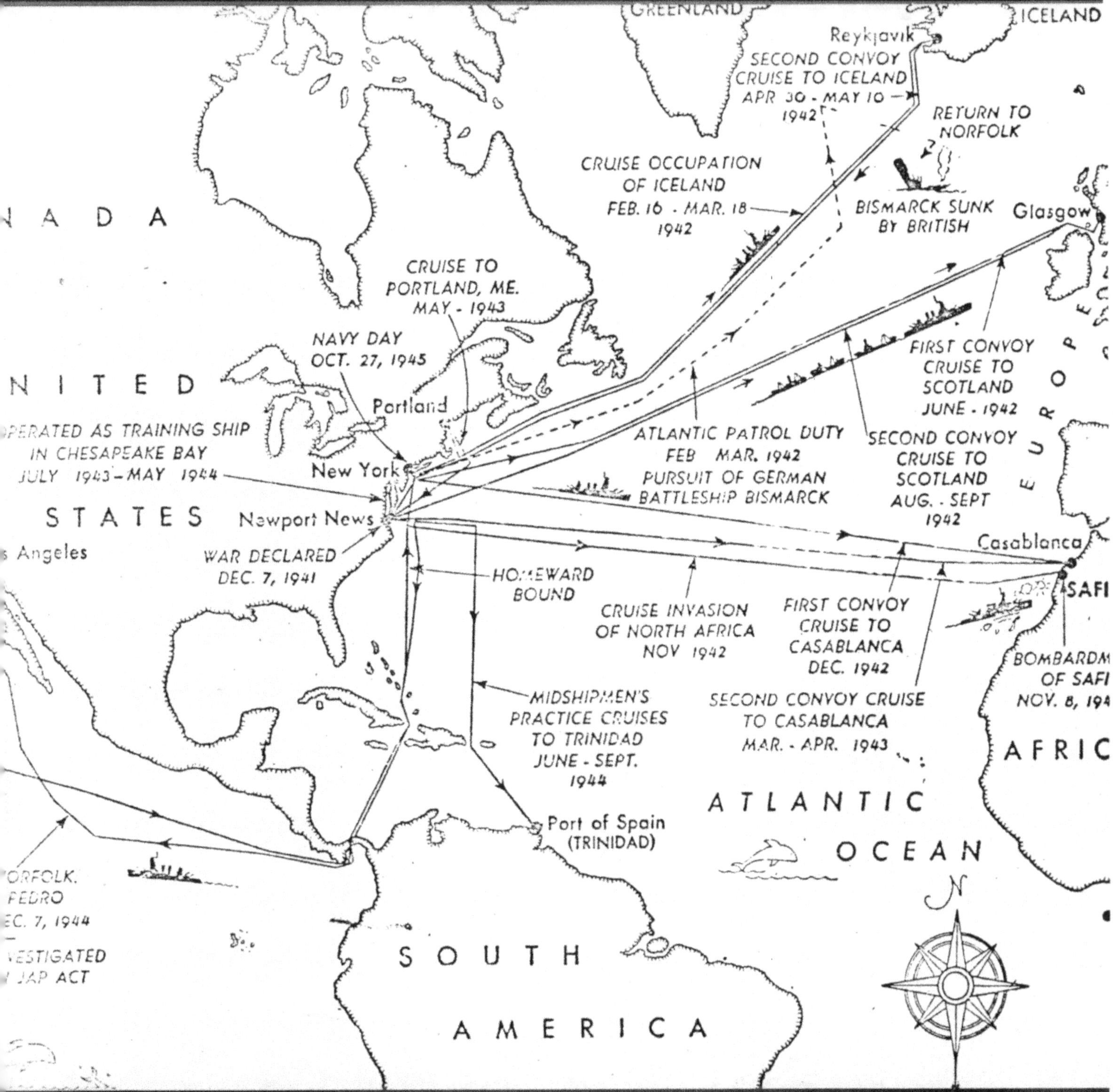
GREENLAND
ICELAND
Reykjavik
SECOND CONVOY CRUISE TO ICELAND APR 30 - MAY 10 1942
RETURN TO NORFOLK
CRUISE OCCUPATION OF ICELAND FEB. 16 - MAR. 18 1942
BISMARCK SUNK BY BRITISH
Glasgow
CRUISE TO PORTLAND, ME. MAY - 1943
NAVY DAY OCT. 27, 1945
FIRST CONVOY CRUISE TO SCOTLAND JUNE - 1942
EUROPE
Portland
PERATED AS TRAINING SHIP IN CHESAPEAKE BAY JULY 1943 - MAY 1944
ATLANTIC PATROL DUTY FEB MAR. 1942 PURSUIT OF GERMAN BATTLESHIP BISMARCK
SECOND CONVOY CRUISE TO SCOTLAND AUG. - SEPT 1942
New York
Newport News
Casablanca
SAFI
WAR DECLARED DEC. 7, 1941
HOMEWARD BOUND
CRUISE INVASION OF NORTH AFRICA NOV 1942
FIRST CONVOY CRUISE TO CASABLANCA DEC. 1942
SECOND CONVOY CRUISE TO CASABLANCA MAR. - APR. 1943
MIDSHIPMEN'S PRACTICE CRUISES TO TRINIDAD JUNE - SEPT. 1944
ATLANTIC OCEAN
Port of Spain (TRINIDAD)
SOUTH AMERICA
N
NADA
NITED STATES
s Angeles
AFRIC
ORFOLK. FEDRO EC. 7, 1944
VESTIGATED JAP ACT

USS NEW YORK (BB-34)

The Old Lady of the Sea

Turner Publishing Company
Paducah, Kentucky

Turner Publishing Company
412 Broadway • P.O. Box 3101
Paducah, KY 42002-3101
(270) 443-0121

Copyright © 2002 Turner Publishing Company.
This book or any part thereof may not be reproduced
without the written consent of the author.

ISBN 978-1-63026-945-6
Library of Congress Control Number: 2002104540

Turner Publishing Company Staff:
Editor: Herbert C. Banks II
Designer: Tyranny J. Bean

Printed in the United States of America.
Limited Edition.

Contents

Message from the Publisher 4

History of the American Battleship 5

USS New York (BB-34) History 27

Stories from the Deck 53

USS New York (BB-34) Shipmates 79

USS New York Shipmate Taps 93

Index 95

A MESSAGE FROM THE PUBLISHER

Among the most famous battleships in the history of the United States, the USS New York (BB-34) is certainly one of the most colorful. From her commissioning in 1914, to her decommissioning in 1948, and later her eight-hour pounding by ships and planes carrying out full scale battle maneuvers, she stood the test of time and proved her worthiness as a sea going vessel for the United States Navy.

This book is dedicated to those of you who proudly served aboard "The Grand Lady of the Fleet" and defended those persecuted by aggression over the decades. It was you, the veterans, who selflessly gave yourselves, heart and soul, and risked your lives. It was you, through your actions, who created the history of the USS New York that is held in such high esteem today. It is through this book that your stories and memories may forever live for future generations to learn.

I would like to thank all of you who submitted your photographs, stories, and personal biographies for inclusion in this history book. I would like to personally thank Mr. H.R. "Shorty" Reynolds for efforts in making this publication possible. I would like to also thank Mr. Kermit Bonner for his guided help in documenting the ship's written history. May God bless America and especially the military veteran.

Dave Turner
President,
Turner Publishing Company

HISTORY OF THE AMERICAN BATTLESHIP

Despite all of the written and spoken descriptions of a battleship, there remains for those who have experienced the sight, sound and service aboard one, a chasm of incompleteness in trying to tie a description and the experience together. No matter how enthusiastic or long the descriptions, words never seem to be enough to capture the actual feeling of being in or around a battleship. It is one of those situations whereby the description always ends with I wish you were there," or "I wish you could have seen her," an experience somewhat similar to trying to describe your best girl with a picture that doesn't say it all.

In attempting to capture this elusive feeling, one can, at best, try to imagine an early morning watch-stander, scanning the ocean and breathing a sigh of relief as the early morning fog begins to break and dissipate. However, he continues to look into the fog, not for what he sees but what he begins to sense. He is able to pick out light fog patches, but what he notices are shades intermixed, light and darker shades of gray together. Gradually, the darker patches blend into one form. Then, with the parting of the fog or the lightening of the day, the watch-stander not knowing which, he sees it: first just a ship's bow steaming through the fog bank, into the light, it grows and grows until " . . .look at her will you!" is thought before said. The ship gliding gracefully grows in the sight and mind of the watch-stander. He begins to feel he is in the presence of some sleek, imposing monolith as its size fills his vision. In almost slow motion it steams — power and force combined, a relaxed being with all its strengths ready to take on the unknown. The young man's senses are not yet segmenting what he sees into gun masts or men. What he sees is a unified being, overwhelming the mind and senses. He perceives a force of integrated men and machinery, together projecting a presence of majestic power on both an emotional and physical level. It is in those fleeting moments that one can fully understand the true meaning of a battleship and all that it stands for.

The Early Days

The battleship of today is a concept of antiquity, when men and societies, later, nations, had to defend themselves from each other. The battleship has also been a marvel of technological progress in man's search for security.

The free use of the sea came into question when the first trade or merchant vessels appeared. The attempt to create a dual use for a sailing vessel, to trade and to fight was successfully developed and practiced for a number of years. However, there are indications that long before the birth of Christianity, the distinction in construction and use of merchant and warships was established.

In the beginning, the most effective of warships was propelled primarily by oarsmen, supplemented by a sail. Particularly in the Mediterranean, the oarsmen of these crafts allowed the ships' movements and speed to be less dependent upon external variables such as weather, tides and the variable winds. Additionally, a ship propelled by oarsmen was better able to make use of a key weapon developed at that time, the ram, because their independent propulsion system allowed them greater maneuverability in the sea battles. This "main battery" was to be supplemented with Greek fire (flaming pitch shot from tubes during early Mediterranean shipping) as its secondary system, along with spearmen and archers.

The first major change made in sea warfare was that made by the Romans during their Punic Wars against the Carthageans which spanned 264 BC to 202 BC. Never known as seafarers, the Romans were quick to modify sea tactics to make use of their strongest weapon, the Roman soldier. They bypassed the use of the ram and Greek fire and devised a new weapon to fit their needs, a "corvus," which was, simply, a bridge. The bridge was devised with a large nail on its end. In battle, the bridge was lowered on an enemy's ship, fixing the ship into position, and providing the means for the Roman troops to board the enemy ship. This allowed them to utilize their best battle strength, fighting hand-to-hand at close quarters. These new tactics helped clear the sea of enemy ships and enabled Rome to conduct a successful invasion of Carthage, removing it as a threat to Roman dominance in the Mediterranean. This was an early example of the importance of useful and efficient vessels for sea battles.

Following the Punic Wars, the Romans returned to the use of oarsmen in their ships. Some ships were built with more than one level of oarsmen, still supplemented by sails. The largest were called "triremes." The use of these ships peaked in the sea battle of Actium, a battle of Roman versus Roman for political control. The result of the peace that followed this culmination of years of sea battles and weapon development brought a reduction in the use and development of warships. This type of escalation and cutback response in weapons and equipment for battles continues today.

During the interim years, a vessel called the "galley ship" came into dominance as the primary type of warship. Employed in the Battle of Lepanto in 1571, it remained primarily a combination of oarsmen and sails, but it incorporated up to three mast and sails to provide additional speed. In a way, the galley ship was a prototype of three-masted sailing ships, which remained as the primary means of ship propulsion until the invention and use of steam power in the 1800s.

The evolution of "war ships" to the sole use of sail and the appearance of the term "ships of the line" were also to accompany advancements in the areas of armor and armaments. The use of wood resulted in a dependence on a thicker type of wood, which provided the greatest protection for ship and man. The average thickness to be used was approximately 1.5 meters.

In the area of armaments, the introduction of gunpowder enabled a quantum leap from Greek fire, spearmen and archers, to the guns developed along with gunpowder. Guns were muzzle-loaded, smooth bore and fired solid balls. These new weapons in turn affected the road to standardized tactics, which were to vary in accordance with the size and placement of guns throughout a warship. Common sense finally resulted in the broadside arrangement of guns aboard major warships. Early propellant charges required that ships come close aside so the balls fired could at least hit the other ship.

Progress in shipbuilding and armaments led to multi-deck ships with larger guns. These changes, single deck or up to three decks, and the increase in the number and size of the guns carried aboard ship, eventually led to more formal ship titles and designations. A "sloop" carried all of her guns (12 to 20) on one deck. A "frigate" had two decks and mounted an average of 40 guns. A "ship of the line," the largest and most powerful of warships at that time, had three decks and 70 or more guns.

The "ship of the line" was a class of ship that evolved out of the tactical formations used by warships in sea battles. In brief, the opposing fleets would most often form into parallel lines, broadside to each other. When in reach of each other, they would fire away. The objective was to put the best or what was considered the most deadly and hence the most effective ship or ships on the line. Under these circumstances, the smaller ships provided support and supplies. A ship or ships worthy of being "on the line" by necessity had to be the best a nation could provide to defend it and defeat those ships of its opponent. Today's battleships are considered the direct descendants of these "ships of the line."

The use of ships of the line served to reinforce the idea that warships should, for appreciable periods of time, be capable of performing operations out of sight of land and away from their homeport. These ships came to be built so that they would be at home on the sea and unlike merchant vessels, they would be able to function in such a way that the sea, extremes in weather permitting, was not to be an enemy, but the arena in which a threat to a nation's security could be defeated.

The age of mercantilism and imperialism gave a special emphasis to the need for secure trade routes and freedom of the seas. The growing awareness of the potential of the sea as an avenue of commerce was beginning to provide the motivation for standing national fleets and the continued improvement of the ships of the line. A nation's ability to construct and maintain ships of the line became, in time, one of the prime indicators of a nation's wealth, its people's standard of living, and its military power. All of these factors contributed towards the determination of a nation's position or standing among the world of nations, hence the importance and emphasis placed upon the manufacturing and maintenance of these great ships.

AMERICAN INTRODUCTION

American independence and initial growth was free from a major dependence upon the sea. Our War for Independence, as well as the War of 1812, found us hindered by the lack of capital ships, but our growth continued to be chiefly supported by internal trade and growth. However, the War of 1812 did increase our awareness, for a time, of the need for capital ships and their relationship to national security. As a result of this awareness, three ships of the line were built: the USS *Independence*, the USS *Franklin*, and the USS *Washington*.

The USS *Independence*, a 74-gun ship of the line, backed up the American naval activity against the Barbary pirates in the Middle East. The presence of American warships in the Middle East fulfilled the primary role of the United States Navy, as the newly created Board of Navy Commissioners and the secretary of the Navy established it. This principle role of the American Navy was to be the protection of United States' maritime commerce. Also, the Navy was to protect the American seacoast and coastal waters in cooperation with the United States Army.

During the period of 1838-1840 and through 1853, the United States Navy explored the seas and oceans and established friendly relations with a number of nations they reached, around the world. The United States' association with China, Japan, and its exploration of the Pacific Ocean laid the basis for the future need and employment of capital ships (ships of the line, now the battleship), to support and protect America's growing interests and presence in the Pacific area.

CHANGES

The early and mid-1800s was to be a period of significant change in the armor, armaments and capabilities of ships of the line. The genius and efforts of James Watt, who invented the first practical steam engine, and Robert Fulton, who was able to apply it in the propulsion of ships, opened the door to an extensive number of inventions.

One invention followed another in almost rapid succession: the explosive shell by Henri Paixhans, the propeller by Joseph Ressel, the French use of armor, the rifle gun by William Armstrong and its adaptation for shipboard use, the use of the steam screw, the fabrication of turrets and others; all led to a break with the past and the eventual genesis of the battleship. The critical areas of concern in the construction of battleships were their armament, armor propulsion, personnel and tactics. Each area was equally important, and the measure of a ship's effectiveness had to be a balanced integration of these elements to provide the most efficient and effective battleship.

The introduction and adaptation of new inventions into the ship construction was often slow and costly. The use of computers and math models to simulate conditions and standards was not available to those developers. People did their best, but often it was a disaster that indicated there was a problem. One such incident occurred after the construction and launching of the *Indiana, Massachusetts* and *Oregon*, it became apparent during their firing trials that the main turrets were not balanced, and the ships listed when all guns were pointed abeam. Fortunately, despite these setbacks, progress continued to be made, and the battleships grew in size and capabilities.

Armament

The armament of a battleship was designed to provide the vessel the most powerful "hitting" power possible. The objective was to destroy any enemy ship as quickly and with the greatest distance separating them as possible. As guns progressed from solid shot muzzle loading smooth bore guns to explosive shell breech loading, rifled guns, their resulting increase in size and blast effect caused a constant trade off between armor, speed, tactics, and radius of action.

As the main guns of American battleships increased in size to 16- inch, 45 caliber guns, their weight and blast characteristics determined their number and placement aboard ship. In order to meet the objective of concentrating the fire of all of the major guns of a ship on one target simultaneously, the center line placement of the main battery of guns was the result of trial and error type experiences. They were fighting ships with more guns than American battleships, but these foreign ships were unable to bring all of their guns to bear at once.

Another consideration in the selection of guns was the necessity to mix dissimilar caliber guns in order to have appropriate responses for different threats. Gradually it became necessary for battleships to engage and defeat ships of lesser tonnage and capabilities. This required a ship to be outfitted with not only guns for the largest of warships (battleships) but also guns for medium to small ships such as cruisers, destroyers and torpedo boats. One smaller ship or a combination of smaller ships could pose a serious threat to an ill-armed battleship, regardless of its size. Guns on the United States ships, at one time or another, included 6-inch, 8-inch, 14-inch and finally, 16-inch guns. In World War II, the Japanese battleship *Yamamoto* was to mount 18-inch guns.

One major threat to battleships that initiated a major armament reorientation was the introduction and increasing use of the attack and fighter airplanes, torpedo planes and dive-bombers. To meet this new menace, battleships increased their secondary weapons inventory and added a number of 40mm and 20mm. In response to today's threats of new weapons including the versatile jet aircraft and missiles, battleships have been armed recently with their own inventory of gattling guns and missiles.

A major characteristic of the battleship that permitted these gun changes was their structural strength and the layout of compartments. The soundness of the original, basic battleship's structure is confirmed today in the USS New Jersey, the USS *Iowa*, the USS *Missouri*, and the USS *Wisconsin*. All have continued to provide an excellent platform for the modernization necessary in order to meet the continually changing threat pattern and systems.

The modern armament of American battleships began with the USS *Indiana* (BB-1). Her armaments included: main - (4) 13"/35 guns, (8) 8"/35 guns and, (4) 6"/40 guns; secondary - (20) pdr. (6) 1 pdr. and (6) 18" surface torpedo tubes. Development of Tennessee Class battleships no longer included torpedo tubes. A major change was reflected in the Iowa Class battleships. These class of ships mounted: main - (9) 16"/50 guns; secondary - (20) 5'/38 guns, (15) to (50) 20mm, and (20) quad 40mm guns. The latest gunning improvement was represented in the USS *New Jersey* (BB-62) of the Iowa Class battleships. The USS *New Jersey* mounts (9) 16"/50 guns, (12) 5"/38 guns in twin mounts, (4) 20mm Phalanx Gattling guns, over 30 Tomahawk missiles, (16) Harpoon anti-ship missiles and (8) 50 cal machine guns. This is obviously an extensive and imposing array of offensive/defensive weapons to meet the most sophisticated of enemy threats.

Supplementary to the armament of the early battleships was the assignment of one to three observation aircraft. Until the use of radar and more advanced fire control systems, these aircraft were the extended eyes of the battleship. Their use and importance to the ship was clearly demonstrated repeatedly in the invasions carried out by American forces in the Pacific and in Europe during the World War II. These planes provided fire support requests and results to the battleships in order to knock out the enemy forces, shore guns and installations. The coordination and effectiveness of the team, pilots and gunners saved the lives of many American Marine and Army troops.

Armor

A ship's armor was that element set aside for the general protection or survival of the ship and crew in combat. The armor carried on board, and its subsequent placement throughout the battleship had a direct impact on the endurance, speed and the offensive/defensive capabilities of a vessel. The ultimate use of armor on a battleship was to maintain the fighting ability of the ship and men aboard her as long as they could inflict damage on an enemy. The common placement of armor was as a belt along the battleship's water line, bow to stern. Thickness of the armor varied 12 to 18 inches and the belt extended 6 to 9 feet above and below the water line.

Also, additional armor of varying thickness protected the battleship's main armament, magazines, propulsion and control systems. Double bottoms and blisters as protection against mines and torpedoes supplemented armor. Double bottoms consisted of a series of small, linked compartments. The areas were empty or storage areas for fuel. Their construction was directed towards absorbing the explosive damage of enemy weapons while still maintaining the basic integrity of the battleship, allowing its continued function.

Armor was also carried on the ship's top deck as protection against enemy aircraft or high angle fire from other battleships. The thickness varied on several of the top decks, being specially designed to absorb as much explosive force as possible without damage to the receiving ship. The American battleship carried fewer armors than the battleships of other nations. On the American ships, what armor they carried was heaviest amid ship and less on the bow and stern areas.

Propulsion

The growth in propulsion systems initially served to free the impact of wind and sea conditions on the employment of combat and tactics of a battleship. In most instances this continued to be the case, unless a battleship found itself supporting an aircraft carrier. The need for carriers to head into the wind or chase the wind in order to launch its aircraft was a nightmare to the navigators aboard all ships in the support group trying to maintain their ship's correct position in formation. During carrier flight operations, the first surface ship objective was not to get run over by a carrier at flank speed turning into the wind for a quick launch or recovery of aircraft.

The use and development of steam power provided increased maneuverability and speed to battleships. As part of the integration of speed, armor and armament, speed was sometimes sacrificed to increase one or both of the other elements.

Propulsion of the early American battleships was provided by coal, which was converted to steam-driven expansion-reciprocating engines. Coal was used in the *Indiana, Iowa, Kearsarge* (the only battleship class not named after a state), *Illinois, Maine, Virginia, Connecticut, South Carolina, Delaware, Florida, Wyoming* and *New York* classes of battleships. Actual tons of coal ranged from the USS *Indiana* at 1640 tons to the USS *New York* at 2850 tons. Coal continued to be used in American battleships through 1910.

As the size and ability of American battleships to carry coal increased, so did the operational requirements for the battleships. American penetration into the pacific region, particularly after the Spanish-American War, demanded the increased presence of American battleships. The experience of President Roosevelt's "Great White Fleet," 16 battleships traveling around the world, highlighted the need for coal refueling stations throughout the pacific area. This need further motivated additional improvements, which led to the introduction of steam turbine systems and turbo-electric systems.

The commissioning of the USS *Nevada* (BB-36) in February of 1916 introduced the substitution of fuel oil for coal. The USS *North Carolina* (BB-55) was a good example of the improvements made. The battleship had eight Babcock and Wilcox boilers, which supplied steam to four sets of General Electric, geared turbines for a total output of 121,000 horsepower. The power was transferred to four shafts and each shaft turned a four-bladed propeller. The inboard propellers were 15 feet; the two outboard were 16 feet. In addition to these propellers, electric motors also operated off of the main propulsion system. Electric motors were used to power everything from elevating the ship's guns and running radar to the ship's electric lights.

THE MEN

The most important variable factored into the equation of what determined the effectiveness of a battleship was the crew. The experiences derived from the length of time that battleships have been around and their performance in battle allow one to conclude that in many cases, the crew was the difference between the success or failure in a battle. It is the integration of skills; machinery and men's wills that make a battleship a fighting ship.

The number of officers and men assigned to operate a battleship varied from 32 officers and 444 enlisted men assigned to the USS *Indiana* (BB-1) to the designated compliment of 117 officers and 1,804 men of the USS *New Jersey* (BB-62). Tied to these numbers was the flip side of "manning" these ships. This is the Navy's organizational responsibility to provide the training programs, time and devices to equip the officers and the men to man the ship, with the knowledge to run the battleship and fight their enemies. World War I and World War II were to tax the system and individuals to the limit, but their results always met the needs of the Fleet.

The advancement of weapon systems has multiplied their complexity and cost. The old "on the job training" did not fit the bill to insure that an individual or a ship was qualified for operational duty. Very often, the ship's system required that the theory as well as the operation of a weapon be combined in training.

The officer complement required training in supervision and interpretation of man and equipment in all of the ship's divisions. An indication of the crew's required skills is illustrated by this sampling of ratings in Figure 1.

Figure 1

Boatswain's Mate	(BM)
Boiler Technician	(BT)
Dental Technician	(DT)
Disbursing Clerk	(DK)
Electrician's Mate	(EM)
Electronic's Technician	(ET)
Electronic's Warfare Technician	(EWT)
Engineman	(EN)
Fire Control Technician	(FT)
Gas Turbine Systems Technician	(GS)
Gunner's Mate	(GM)
Hospital Corpsman	(HM)
Hull Maintenance Technician	(HT)
Instrumentman	(IM)
Intelligence Specialist	(IS)
Interior Communications Electrician	(IC)
Machinery Repairman	(MR)
Machinist's Mate	(MM)
Master at Arms	(MA)
Mess Management Specialist	(MS)
Missile Technician	(MT)
Operations Specialist	(OS)
Opticalman	(OM)
Personnel Man	(PN)
Quartermaster	(QM)
Signalmen	(SM)

The listing reflects the changes from sail to steam and coal to oil. Additionally it delineates the rapid expansion of electronics and its expansion throughout the ship, be it in communications or the launching and control of missiles. The introduction of computers and the computerization of figuratively "anything that moves" added the Data Processing Technician (DP) and the Data Systems Technician (DS) ratings to answer the ever-changing needs aboard a battleship.

The success of a battleship in combat was the measure of its crew. The role of battleships in post-World War II conflicts such as Korea, Vietnam and Lebanon, continue to reflect the competence and the adaptability of officers and crew as the battleships were forced to meet an increasing number of threats from various sources against the security of the United States and her allies.

There are a number of ways to appreciate how battleship personnel feel about themselves, their ship, and other units within the Navy and the world in general. One way to be fully informed about their various opinions is to state or imply inferiority in their ship, crewmates or officers, or the superiority of any other Navy branch. The response would most likely confirm the characterization of battleship sailors as colorful in manner and language alike. However, it would leave no doubt that this group of men is an entity to themselves and cannot be replaced.

That battleship men have a special bond was verified by the number of requests to meet the call to the recommissioning of the USS *New Jersey*. To many, the battleship represented the best of the "real Navy." The size and complexity of a battleship did not accept but the best from each individual. It was not a question of convenience or just looking good. A man's survival, whether in combat or not, depended upon his performance while aboard ship. Misuse of or inattention when using equipment or a weapon system could, in an instant, take one or several men's lives, hence the phrase, "The book was written in blood."

Despite being a tight ship run on the spit-and-polish principle, the battleship was often the only home a sailor had; the concept "you take care of her and she'll take care of you" prevailed. Although the life did fill the advertisement, "Join and see the world," it was not a pleasure cruise. Aboard ship there were many attempts at recreation, but "chow" was the pivot of the day. In some ports it earned a quick return to the ship before proceeding with liberty.

The positive results of discipline and the working integration of officers and men were demonstrated time and time again through wars and police actions. Whether providing fire support for others or fighting to save the ship, the job was done. At Pearl Harbor, perhaps the worst of possible Navy nightmares, men on and off duty stood their stations. They took a brutal blow from a highly trained and motivated enemy but was not defeated. World War II ended in victory, but never on the long and tortuous path to this goal did the dedication and performance of the battleship sailor ever slackens. Battleship sailors had to watch the newly heralded carrier ships take the lead, but often those on the carriers and invading on land were grateful for the fire protection and support the battleship's guns and people provided.

TACTICS

An external element, which influenced the performance of a battleship, was the tactics planned for and carried out by the ship. The objective of a battleship was to rush out and take on the enemy's battleship. However, as stated above, the variety of threats a battleship could encounter in times of war required a mix of weapons and an integrated balance of armor, armament and speed. For the most part, the presence of main and secondary gun systems was enough to meet the different surface threats as ably demonstrated by their success in the Spanish-American War.

The first major re-evaluation of the employment of battleships was with the operational use of submarines. Armor and blisters did not seem sufficient to ensure the continued operational employment of battleships in submarine infested waters. The submarine problem was to be countered by providing increased anti-submarine protection through smaller surface craft or through the utilization of battleships in areas outside the effective radius of submarine activity. During World War I, battleships did provide convoy escort duty in company with anti-submarine surface ships. Additionally, when joined to the British home fleet, they provided protection against the possibility of German battleships raiding English coastal areas or Allied convoys, and was able to still operate away from the major submarine threat areas.

The British and German experience in May 1916, in the Battle of Jutland left doubts in the minds of supporters and critics as to the use of battleships. What seemed to have been overlooked was an awareness of the adaptability of the role of the battleship to fit the needs of England or Germany. Often overlooked was that the English had a strategic victory in neutralizing the German Fleet as a threat to its own coast or to the millions of tons of equipment and the men travelling across the Atlantic. The success of a weapon can be judged in many ways and possibly the role of the battleship in World War I deserved more study to determine the true strengths and weaknesses of the use of this particular "weapon." The disaster of the English employment of battleships in Turkish waters did little to enhance the reputation of their use.

The result of World War I on battleship tactics was that battleships were only used primarily to balance the combatants. There was little or no interest demonstrated in making battleships a positive and crucial element in the overall mix of a nation's arms necessary to defeat an enemy. There were not any tacticians like J.E.C. Fuller, B.H. Liddel Hart, or Heinz Guderian advocating new battleship tactics. Instead, in the interim years of 1918 to 1938, battleship tactics and development proceeded inversely to the civilian populations' desire to outlaw war following the devastation left by World War I. As many failed to appreciate the critical and tenuously balanced international environment around them, the military also failed to appreciate the scientific advances that would eventually have impact upon the role and use of various weapons, including the battleship. These scientific advances, especially in the fields of radar and aircraft use and performance, would have determinative and long-term effects in the next world war.

After being initially caught off-guard and unprepared at the beginning of World War II, the thinking of battleship utilization was to be overwhelmed by a rapid series of disasters experienced by England and the United States in the early stages of World War II. In one rapid blow, the loss at Pearl Harbor of the USS *Arizona* (BB-39), the subsequent loss of the USS *Oklahoma* (BB-

37), and the damage to the USS *California* (BB-44), the USS *West Virginia* (BB-48), the USS *Pennsylvania* (BB-38), the USS *Tennessee* (BB-43), the USS *Maryland* (BB-46) and the USS *Nevada* (BB-36) put a dark cloud over the complete spectrum of battleship employment. The battleship itself and its planned utilization were initially to receive modifications and employment changes almost on a day-to-day basis. The roles it filled as anti-aircraft gunship, shore bombardment support, heavy escort for supply lines, and secondary backup to the carrier groups were self-made: as vacuums appeared, battleships took up the slack and performed whatever job was necessary. The modification of several battleships with new and updated weapon systems today supports the speculation that had research continued to be applied to the battleship during the 1918 to 1938 period, their use may have been significantly enhanced at a much earlier date.

Currently, the recent continued loss of American oversea areas to base surfaces and the increasing spread of terrorist tactics by a number of Second and Third World nations make the continued use and appearance of battleships in those areas a viable working option to protect the numerous and varied interests the United States has a broad and closer to home.

THE BATTLESHIP IS ARRIVING

In examining the actual development of the battleship in America, it appears to have received its greatest push from the steam warship demologos which could be considered the earliest prototype for the modern battleship. The Civil War provided early examples for the use of armored warships, steam and turrets. However, the end of the War Between the States saw the loss of the natural interest in battleships or military development in general due to the absence of need.

What aroused the American interest in the battleship subject again was not the wars in Europe, but the American concern with its natural growth and expansion and its "Manifest Destiny." After the Civil War, the country continued to expand until reaching the boundary of the Pacific Ocean. Not to be outdone by the actions of the major European nations, that, in the 1900s, were establishing overseas possessions, the United States looked to the Caribbean and the Pacific areas for possible expansion. The interest of the United States in a strong navy was further stimulated by the publication and dissemination throughout the world of a book *The Influence of Sea Power upon History, 1660-1783,* by Alfred Thayer Mahan, an American naval officer. The book provided a valid summation of cause and effect studies of international trade, national growth and national security. It emphasized the impact of trade, the availability of natural resources and the need for a powerful, if not overwhelming, naval force for a nation to become and remain a world power. The powers of Europe were soon concerned with strengthening their ability to guarantee the security of their trade routes and overseas possessions. Together these sources provided the natural resources to feed Europe's ever growing and expanding industries. Natural self-interest demanded the best naval forces possible, and at the top of the list of requirements was the need for the biggest, most powerful and heaviest battleships possible.

The United States quickly decided that, to act in its best interest and to manufacture the best ships possible to fit its needs, it would be necessary to assimilate what progress had been made in armor, armament and propulsion systems by England, France, Italy and Russia, and to incorporate these advances into their designs. Three battleship keels were laid in 1891: the USS *Indiana* (BB-1), the USS *Massachusetts* (BB-2), and the USS *Oregon* (BB-3). The keels of two other ships, the USS *Texas* and the USS *Maine* were laid in 1888 and 1889. Both were designated second-class battleships and launched prior to BB-1 through BB-3. Just prior to the Spanish-American War, America was to add the USS *Iowa* (BB-4) to its inventory of battleships.

During the time these ships were built, a number of changes occurred. The USS *Texas* and USS *Maine* had an average displacement of 6,000 to 7,000 tons. The Indiana Class averaged 11,000 tons. Armament increased from 8 main armament guns and 22 secondary guns of the USS *Maine* to 18 main armament guns and 28 secondary guns on the USS *Iowa*. The main effect of the USS *Maine* was its role in triggering the war between the United States and Spain. When the battleship blew up while in the port of Havana, Cuba, the blame was laid at the door of Spain. The USS *Indiana* and the USS *Iowa* were ordered to positions to meet the anticipated threat posed by the arrival of the Spanish Fleet in the Americas. The USS *Oregon* successfully circumnavigated South America to reinforce the Atlantic Fleet. On 3 July 1898, American battleships, minus the USS *Massachusetts*, met and in a running battle, defeated the Spanish Fleet in the Battle of Santiago.

Although the Spanish-American War was not a masterpiece of organization, one item did stand out, and this, namely, was the accuracy of the United States' battleship gunners. Whatever the condition of the Spanish Fleet, the fact that the American ships were devastatingly effective in hitting what they aimed for, helped to convince the Spanish that surrender was their only option under those type of conditions.

The Russo-Japanese War of 1904-1905 helped to maintain our interest in battleship production, primarily because of the beating the Russian Fleet took at the hands of the Japanese. Japan's entrance on the scene as a naval power shocked the western world. During the period 1905 through 1914, the United States was to launch 20 battleships.

World War I

During World War I, the major event for battleships was the Battle of Jutland between the English and German fleets. The results of the battle served the English objective of keeping the German Fleet in port for the remainder of the war. To the Americans, it was a poor showing of English sea power. English propaganda in America had been too successful about the English's Fleet supposed ability to destroy the German Fleet. The lack of a clear-cut naval victory stimulated America to authorize the building of 10 additional battleships if it became necessary for the U.S. to face the German Fleet.

American battleship commitment to World War I included nine coal burning and three oil burning battleships. The coal burners included the USS *New York* (BB-34), the USS *Wyoming* (BB-32), the USS *Florida* (BB-30), and the USS *Delaware* (BB-28), they were assigned to serve with the British Home Fleet and Scapa Flow because of the availability of coal and the lack of oil. The USS *Nevada* (BB-36), USS *Oklahoma* (BB-37), and the USS *Utah* (BB-31) were assigned operational responsibilities off the coast of southern Ireland in Bantry Bay from September to November of 1918. They were to prevent any German surface ships from attacking American troop or supply ships enroute to England. The remaining American battleships performed escort duty with the American Atlantic Fleet or were held in reserve off the American coast.

Changes

The improvements in battleship construction continued from 1908 through the entire war period. This was demonstrated with the USS *New Hampshire* (BB-25), commissioned in 1908. Her construction consisted of: length, 456', beam, 76', displacement, 16,000 tons, main armament 24 guns of three varying sizes, 22 secondary guns, 12" armor, submerged torpedo tubes, and a speed of 18 knots using coal for fuel. In comparison, the USS *Pennsylvania* (BB-38), commissioned in 1906 consisted of: length, 608', beam, 97', displacement, 31,400 tons; and initially outfitted with 12 main guns of 14" single size, 22 secondary guns of 5"/51, 18" armor, and a speed 21 knots using a turbine drive fueled with an oil propulsion system.

Of main importance were the differences in size, armament, armor, and propulsion systems. Difficulties surmounted during this period included the damaging effect of gun blasts by larger 8" guns on smaller sized guns and the discontinued use of two-story turrets in the Connecticut class. The reduction in the varying number of gun sizes in turn reduced the multiplicity of magazines aboard ship. Valuable modifications in the gun area were the changes to ammunition hoists, modified in 1908. They were disconnected into segmented stages to bring up ammunition from the magazines. The change was to prevent the possibility of burning gasses or debris falling directly into the ammunition handling area.

The switch from coal to oil began with the USS *Nevada* and it proved a boost not only to the battleship's efficient use of fuel, but a boost to the men's morale; it had always been an "all hands party" for taking on coal!

Matching the developments of battleship construction was the growing organization to support the new ships. New machines and new weapons were always more complex, and the Navy was successful in providing the programs and devices needed to supply the required training.

LET DOWN

American interest at the end of World War I was to make the American Navy the worlds most powerful. The continued development of the Japanese Fleet had begun to cast a shadow over the Western and Central Pacific. Unfortunately, the end to this American dream and the meeting of the Japanese threat was to be the beginning of the post-war depression. Congress and the country at large looked to economic recovery, not military build-up. Pacifism rode the back of the depression. There was no war; therefore the money available had to be used for helping people, not in developing better ways in which to kill them.

Right or wrong, the mood of the country was to be fertile ground for the Washington Conference of November 1921, and the following 9-and 5- power agreements of 1921-1922. The agreements put the brake on the construction started in 1920 on the USS *South Dakota* (BB-49), the USS *Indiana* (BB-50), USS *Montana* (BB-51), USS *North Carolina* (BB-52), USS *Iowa* (BB-53), and the USS *Massachusetts* (BB-54). All were cancelled for construction in 1922.

During the Hoover Administration not a single combat vessel was built. Peace was to be negotiated. It was to be much later when we admitted, "the king wore no clothes."

Congressional Acts of 1934, 1936, and 1938 provided authorization for building capital ships only as replacements and only if the president determined a need. The Congressional Act of May 1938 finally increased the allowed tonnage of capital ships to 105,000 tons. This came only after Germany and Japan had begun building their capital ships above the 1921-1922 agreements. In 1940, the Navy was allowed a further increase of 1,350,000 tons. The keel of the first American battleship to be completed since World War I was the USS *North Carolina* (BB-55) in 1937.

THE IN BETWEEN YEARS

In the 1930s and 1940s, the lid was gradually taken off the size of a battleship. In 1934, Italy placed the first order for a 35,000-ton battleship. This was followed by German re-entry into the building race with the SCHARNHORST class battleship. In the United States, the second Vinson Act in May 1938, authorized the construction of additional battleships: the South Dakota class (35,000 tons), and the Iowa class (45,000 tons). By 1938, Britain continued to build ships of 45,000 tons, but opted for 16" guns, as the Americans had beginning with the USS *Colorado* (BB-45) in 1919. In the closing phases of World War II, the existence of Japan's super battleships became known with the appearance of two YAMATO classes battleships. Each had a displacement of 64,000 tons, and came with 18.1" guns.

An evaluation of the Italian use of battleships was extremely limited due to their poor watertight integrity and battle-readiness. The performance of Germany's Bismark in sinking *H. M. Hood* and her own end demonstrated the true staying power of battleships. The Bismark, after taking a steering gear casualty, expended all her ammunition, then opened her scuttle valves and set-off explosive charges within the ship. As the English Fleet worked her over, she finally capsized and sank. The English action accelerated her own end, but in the final analysis, it seemed her end was more of her own crew's action. The battleship itself did what it was supposed to do, fight and survive. The actual inner structure of the battleship was pierced one or two times. The ship's tactical employment shares equal blame for her loss with the actions of the enemy.

The English loss of the *Repulse* and the *Prince of Wales*, and the American disaster at Pearl Harbor almost served to bury the battleships and their uses to the pages of history. The American and later Allied, use of battleships as a valued and necessary part of an offensive force in the pacific area was to validate their need and worth. The American Pacific Fleet utilized the best of each weapons system, the strong and the weak points of battleships, carriers, cruisers, destroyers, submarines, and support forces, each serving to balance the other. It was the genius of the Americans to appreciate an old rule; the value of the whole is greater than each of its parts. The Americans used this concept and time and again it proved itself both in American use and its misuse by our enemies.

THIS IS NO DRILL

As the United States was walking into World War II, the role call of battleships in December 1941 was: USS *New York* (BB-34), USS *Texas* (BB-35), USS *Arkansas* (BB-33), USS *New Mexico* (BB-40), USS *Mississippi* (BB-41), and USS *Idaho* (BB-42) (operationally a part of the U.S. Atlantic Fleet, and assigned to the conduct of Neutrality Patrols in the North Atlantic.) The USS *Wyoming* (BB-32) was in use as a training ship in Norfolk, Va., and the USS *Colorado* (BB-45) was undergoing a conversion in Puget Sound. The USS *North Carolina* (BB-55), and the USS *Washington* (BB-56), commissioned in April and May of 1941 respectively, were in sea trials.

The remaining battleships were in port at Pearl Harbor and took the brunt of the Japanese sneak attack on 7 December. While the Oklahoma was severely damaged and capsized during the attack, she was up-righted and was enroute to the mainland when she parted her tow and sank. The USS *Nevada* (BB-36) was hit with 1 A/C torpedo and 5 A/C bombs. She sank in harbor mud, but was raised and returned to duty. USS *Oklahoma* (BB-37) capsized, and was later raised but did not return to the Fleet (the *Oklahoma* had been assigned in 1936 to rescue Americans caught in Spain during the Spanish Civil War). The USS *Pennsylvania* (BB-38) was damaged but returned to duty. The USS *Arizona* (BB-39) hit by one A/C torpedo and eight A/C bombs sank, and in 1962 was dedicated as a National Memorial. The USS *Tennessee* (BB-43) was damaged, but returned to duty, as did the USS *California* (BB-44), hit by two A/C torpedoes, and 3 A/C bombs. The USS *Maryland* (BB-46) was hit by two A/C bombs and was repaired and returned to duty, and the USS *West Virginia* was also repaired and returned to duty after being hit by six A/C torpedoes and two A/C bombs.

The events surrounding the disaster at Pearl Harbor will continue to be discussed long after we are all gone. What has and will be agreed upon is the unification of the citizens of the United States behind a single objective - victory over her enemies. The attack also left no doubt in anyone's mind that the role of the battleship in combat was to be forever changed. Unfortunately, what continued to be overshadowed by the changes in roles were the vital contributions battleships did provide in the Pacific and Atlantic theaters of war.

WHAT WE DID (PACIFIC)

The strategic decision to make Europe the primary area of commitment was to allow the pacific area commanders some degree of flexibility in their operations. The plan for Japan, or "the road back", was to conduct flanking attacks on Japanese positions across the Pacific, with the addition of attacks up the center of the flanks — a plan which did not permit Japanese freedom of action with their military forces.

The major pivotal points in recovering lost positions and attacking Japan included General MacArthur operating out of Australia, and Admiral Nimitz attacking from the Central and South Pacific. As General MacArthur advanced his troops, he was able to provide both land-based and naval augmented support for his forces. Admiral Nimitz was required to develop a complete base of operations and support that moved with him at sea. The United States Navy had to develop and protect the largest umbilical cord in history.

The carrier forces served as the points for Admiral Nimitz's actions. The battleships provided both supports for the carriers, and also served as a core of heavy second-line defense for the long train of supporting troopships, repair ships, fuel tankers, and cargo carriers. The success of all future naval actions was to depend on the protected lifeline feeding beans and bullets to the land, sea, subsea, and air operations of Admiral Nimitz. The U.S. Navy's organization was laid over a foundation provided by the battleships.

Once the Fleet's actions began to roll over the Pacific, the Navy was no longer a thin shield of defense. It was a complete combat force in breadth and depth never seen and never imagined by anyone prior to the hostilities. The Central Pacific Forces attacked from Pearl Harbor through the Gilbert, Marshall, and Mariana Islands, through Iwo Jima and Okinawa. The South Pacific Forces worked through Northern New Guinea, the Philippine Islands, and the South China Sea. All forces were homing in on the main islands of Japan.

Prior to the war's end, the battleship force was increased by seven additional ships: USS *South Dakota* (BB-57), USS *Indiana* (BB-58), USS *Massachusetts* (BB-59), USS *Alabama* (BB-60), USS *Iowa* (BB-61), USS *New Jersey* (BB-62), USS *Missouri* (BB-63), and USS *Wisconsin* (BB-64). An additional seven were programmed and work initiated, but they were never completed because of the war's end in 1945.

Following Pearl Harbor, the remaining battleships afloat in the Pacific were assigned escorts and patrols duties along the Eastern Pacific. Point battleships were the USS *Mississippi* (BB-41), and the USS *Maryland* (BB-46) performing either escort or guard duty in the Midway Islands area. By May 1942, and June 1942, the battles of Coral Sea and Midway had been fought. The Coral Sea was the first combat between carrier forces, and although American losses were heavy, it represented the first time a Japanese advance was stopped.

At the Battle of Midway, American forces were outgunned and outnumbered. However, Intelligence provided information on the intentions of the Japanese fleet. The result of superior intelligence, the enemy splitting his forces and the American carriers pressing the issue resulted in a defeat for Japanese ambitions to capture Midway. The Japanese loss of pilots was to restrict their later activities throughout the pacific area. The two naval victories served to motivate American action to take the initiative against the Japanese.

The first step back was to be our attack on Guadalcanal in the Solomon Islands. The battle for the island was to be costly in men and ships. The first surface engagement took place off Savo Island, and the battle was an American disaster with the loss of four heavy cruisers. During 23-24 August 1942 in the Guadalcanal area the USS *North Carolina* (BB-55) was steaming in company with three U.S. carriers; the *Wasp*, the *Saratoga*, and the *Enterprise*. In the exchange of carrier strikes, the USS *Enterprise* was damaged and the Japanese lost a heavy carrier. On 6 September, now a gun ship for the *Wasp* and *Saratoga*, the *North Carolina* shot down six enemy aircraft. However, on 15 September, the *North Carolina* was torpedoed and ordered to return to Pearl for repairs. Further submarine action sunk the *Wasp* and damaged the *Saratoga*. In continued attempts to prevent our being driven off the island, the *Hornet* and the *Enterprise* were committed to attacking the Japanese Fleet. On 24 October, the *Hornet* was sunk, and our last carrier in the area, the *Enterprise*, heavily damaged.

As the Marines fought to hold on to the island, the USS *Washington* (BB-56), and the USS South Dakota (BB-57) arrived. Almost immediately, the USS *South Dakota* took some damage to her bridge, but both battleships became a part of the carrier *Enterprise's* screen. *Enterprise* aircraft began a three-day battle with attacks on a Japanese force including two battleships, the *Hei*, and the *Kirishima*. On the first day, American aircraft heavily damaged the *Hei*, and the shore-based aircraft at Henderson Field later sank her, as the two American battleships raced to engage the Japanese on 14 November. The USS *South Dakota* was disabled off Savo Island with over 30 hits, and two U.S. destroyers were sunk.

The last remaining American capital ship to meet the Japanese forces was the USS *Washington* (BB-56). In the battle that followed, the superior gunnery of the *Washington* sunk one Japanese destroyer and lay waste the battleship *Kirishima*. This action turned the Japanese back and prevented major Japanese reinforcements from landing on Guadalcanal. The USS *Washington* was to be the only American battleship to sink a Japanese battleship. Guadalcanal was declared secure on 9 February 1943. It was to be the first of many examples of sailors, marines, and soldiers obtaining victory by courage, initiative, and never giving in to any doubt of their ultimate success.

The next American move was to regain Attu and Kiska Islands in the Aleutian chain. Attu was the first target and six battleships shelled it. The USS *New Mexico* (BB-40), USS *Mississippi* (BB-41), and USS *Tennessee* (BB-43) provided general fire support, while the USS *Nevada* (BB-36), USS *Pennsylvania* (BB-38), and USS *Idaho* (BB-42) provided direct bombardment fire. The fire support of the battleships drove the Japanese troops in to the mountains. Regrouping, the Japanese staged a banzai charge and were swept away by American fire. The landings several weeks later at Kiska had a pleasant surprise for the troops: the Japanese had left and in their place the Americans found three dogs.

After the Aleutians, the Central Pacific Forces against Betio Island, in the Tarawa Atoll, and Makin Island, launched the next major attack in the Gilbert Island chain, on 21 November 1943. A total of nine battleships were involved in these operations. Four battleships were used against Makin Island, and five, including the flagship, the USS *Maryland* (BB-46), were used against Betio Island. A delay in the scheduled capture of Makin Island and a low tide at Betio Island made the Tarawa landings a near disaster. The battleships *Tennessee, Idaho, Mississippi, North Carolina, New Mexico, Pennsylvania, Colorado,* and *South Dakota* laid in at sometimes less than 8,000 yards for gunnery support of the Marines ashore. At battle's end, some 17 Japanese troops remained alive.

Central Pacific Forces followed quickly with a series of attacks on islands in the Marshall Island chain. By 1944, the battleship forces represented a terrifying array of heavy gun support. Including battleship refitting and battle damage, in 1944, the battleship force in the Marshall Islands was up to 14. Between refitting and invasions, the battleships conducted almost continuous raids throughout the Marshall and Mariana Islands. Between 31 January and 22 February 1944, invasions were launched at Kwajalein, Eniwetok, and Truk Islands. At Kwajalein, the *Tennessee* and *Pennsylvania* laid 1500 yards off the invasion beach and destroyed everything in sight. Some confusion did arise, however, and the *Washington* and the *Indiana* collided, and the Admiral had to shift his flag from the *Washington* to the *North Carolina*.

The Empire State battleship as she passes under the Golden Gate Bridge. She carries a skeleton crew and has been stripped of her up-to-date armaments. She has been prepared for Operation Crossroads and will join some 70 other test ships in the Marshall Islands for the nuclear bomb tests scheduled for July 1946.

USS New York *Seaplane launch in the North Atlantic, 1941. G. Pomeroy in rear cockpit.*

The old battleship gently steams into New York harbor to the cheers of sailors and well wishers. Her tripod masts, 14-inch guns, and ram like bow betray her age, but she still lis a wonderful fighting lady. Updated with radar, she held swa with the best.

The New York *slides under the Golden Gate Bridge and out of San Francisco Harbor for the South Pacific. She is alone in this photo taken on May 2, 1946.*

The old ship has just been subjected to an air burst and an under water explosion that sunk or heavily damaged many other ships. The New York *survived virtually intact and still able to fight. The Atomic bomb was not the doom of the Navy after all. Her next stop would be back to Pearl Harbor for analysis and testing.*

The end of the old lady of the sea, New York, *comes after eight plus hours of systematic bombing, strafing, rocket fire and gun fire from a variety of surface and aircraft. The new 5 inch rocker was tested on the old girl. She held up well, but finally, enough was enough, and late on July 8, 1946, she turned turtle and sank.*

The USS Iowa *(BB-61).*

The USS Indiana *(BB-58).*

The USS California *(BB-44).*

During the invasion of Saipan, conducted 15 June to 9 July, there developed the battle of the Philippine Sea, 19 June — 20 June. The composition of American forces was divided into five groups, four of which contained three or four aircraft carriers. 15 battleships supported the carrier and invasion forces. The list included: the USS *Iowa*, the USS *Massachusetts*, the USS *Tennessee*, the USS *New Jersey*, the USS *North Carolina*, the USS *Indiana*, the USS *Washington*, the USS *California*, the USS *Pennsylvania*, the USS *New Mexico*, USS *Alabama*, the USS *Mississippi*, the USS *Idaho*, the USS *Colorado*, and the USS *Maryland* after her refitting. On 19 June began the greatest carrier battle of the war. The Japanese in one day were to lose 346 aircraft to American aircraft and surface ship support. Considering the number of battleship guns disbursed among our carriers for fire support, the air was heavy with lead.

During the battle, a kamikaze aircraft hit the USS INDIANA. The USS *South Dakota* was hit by a bomber, the USS *California* took a hit from shore fire, and the USS *Tennessee* suffered three shore hits as they supported the Saipan landings. During 21 July to 20 August, our battleships supported landings at Guam and Tinian Islands. Off Tinian Island, the USS *Colorado* was to be hit 22 times by coastal fire.

The battle for Leyte Gulf in support of the Leyte invasion was to be one of the greatest naval actions in history. It consisted of four different battles, and when it was over, Japan no longer had a fighting naval fleet.

The schedule for the next series of actions were October, Leyte; December, Luzon; January 1945, Iwo Jima; and March Okinawa.

Two American Fleets were to be involved in the invasion of the Philippines. The Third Fleet, commanded by Admiral Halsey, included ten new battleships. The Seventh Fleet, commanded by Vice Admiral Kinkaid, was a mixed force of American and Australian forces and also included six battleships. The American battleships included; the *New Jersey, Tennessee, Iowa,*

The USS West Virginia *(BB-48)*.

The USS Wisconsin *(BB-64) and* USS New Jersey *(BB-62)*.

Massachusetts, California, Pennsylvania, New Mexico, West Virginia, Maryland, and the *Colorado.*

At the Leyte invasion, the Japanese committed their combined Fleet. Their Central Force was to travel via the San Bernadino Strait to the Leyte Gulf and attack the American invasion forces. The Japanese Southern Force would transit the Surigao Strait to the Leyte Gulf. The Japanese carrier force, with very few aircraft remaining, really a decoy force, was to draw the Third Fleet north and out of the way.

On 23 October, the Japanese Central Force suffered battle losses to American submarines, and the next day American carrier forces forced the Japanese to retreat. The Japanese Southern Force on 25 October ran into American Forces under Rear Admiral Oldendorf. The American patrol boats, destroyers, and cruisers were distributed along the interior flanks of the Surigao Strait. At the northern end of the strait, where it feeds into the Leyte Gulf, a force of American battleships sat waiting.

The Japanese came under early attack as they entered the strait; guns and torpedoes were launched at the Japanese line of ships. As the Japanese pressed forward, their line of ships were capped by the American battleships in a classic "T", with all battleships concentrating their fire on the Japanese line. Admiral Oldendorf finally ordered firing to cease for fear of Americans hitting each other. The Japanese escaped with one cruiser and one destroyer. The Battle of Surigao Strait was a naval battle without aircraft; it was to be the end of an era.

Admiral Halsey had assumed the Japanese Central Force, like the Southern, no longer a threat and he took his Task Force 38 out after the Japanese carriers. Admiral Halsey, on departing, left the San Bernadino Strait forces without any heavy ship or aircraft support. On 25 October, the Japanese fell on the Americans at San Bernadino. The line up for the Japanese was four battleships, six heavy cruisers, and many destroyers. For the Americans, six escort carriers and several destroyers. In the free-for-all that followed, the Americans sank three enemy cruisers, and so disrupted the Japanese that they withdrew. The Americans lost one escort carrier, the *Gambier Bay*, and one destroyer, the *Johnston*, who took on four Japanese destroyers, and one cruiser in her defense of the escort carriers.

Later American carrier strikes confirmed the Japanese decision to retreat. By now, Halsey had detached the USS *New Jersey* and the USS *Iowa* in an unsuccessful attempts to intercept the Japanese. At the end of four days, the Americans had shattered what remained of the Japanese Navy. The last major weapon to face the American Fleets was the kamikaze pilot. Committed during the Leyte operations, they were so effective that as the Army was completing ground operations, the Navy withdrew its carrier forces for the Luzon operation. Japanese losses for the period included: one large and three light aircraft carriers, three battleships (one of the two largest in the world), two heavy cruisers, four light cruisers, and 12 destroyers.

As the Luzon invasion began, Japanese kamikaze aircraft struck the Fleet. Early in the battle they struck, hitting the battleships *New Mexico* and *California*, and on the November 9, one hit the *Mississippi*. One out of every 33 aircraft attacks sank a ship. It was finally the combined efforts of the third and seventh fleet carriers, that by mid-January 1945 the threat was eliminated.

As an island, Iwo Jima was nothing but volcanic ash, steaming fissures and gorges. The fighting was the first Japanese defense of their homeland. Its need was like that of a number of other islands; to provide landing fields for attacks against mainland Japan.

Even with bombardment support beginning three days early on 16 February from nine battleships sometimes firing from 4,000 yards and less, it still took over 30 days of fighting, and almost 30,000 American and Japanese deaths before we secured the island.

The battleship support continued to consist mainly of the older battleships: the

Arkansas, New York, Texas, Nevada, Idaho, and *Tennessee*. However, three newer battleships joined them in the bombardment support; the *Indiana*, the *Massachusetts*, and the *Missouri*.

The invasion of Okinawa on 1 April 1945 was best summarized by "Americans fighting to stay alive and Japanese fighting to die." Over 30 American naval vessels were to be sunk and over 387 damaged. The Japanese were to deploy the full might of their kamikaze attacks in several massive waves. A kamikaze crashed into the *Maryland* as other battleships began sustaining hits by kamikaze pilots and included the *New York, Nevada, New Mexico, Missouri,* and *West Virginia*. The shore bombardment and anti-aircraft fire support provided by the battleships helped to insure that the Fleet was there to stay until the island was secured.

Following the invasion of Okinawa, the battleships turned their attention to action in the Japanese home waters. Through the bombing of Hiroshima on 6 August and Nagasaki on 9 August with atomic bombs, battleships ranged throughout the Japanese home waters. The battleships in the Japanese home waters included: the USS *Indiana*, the USS *Iowa*, the USS *New Jersey*, the USS Massachusetts the USS *Tennessee*, the USS *North Carolina*, and the USS *Missouri*. It seemed only fitting that on 2 September 1945, the signing of the documents of Japanese surrender would be conducted aboard a battleship, the USS *Missouri* (BB-63), one of the newest battleships in the American Fleet.

WHAT WE DID (EUROPE)

The battleships in the European theater included the USS *Arkansas* (BB-33) initially on-duty off Iceland in 1941, but also serving as escort for 11 convoys between the United States and England. Also performing escort duty was the *New York*, and *Texas*. *Washington* and *Alabama* assignments included escort duty in the Murmansk runs to Russia.

Operation TORCH, on 8 November 1942, the Allied invasion of North Africa, was supported by the *Arkansas* and *New York* in company with the *Massachusetts*. The three U.S. battleships engaged the French battleships *Jean Bart* and *Richelieu* at Casablanca. The *New York* heavily damaged the *Jean Bart*, which remained in port at Casablanca throughout the war. Through 1942 to 1943, the American battleships continued their escort duty from America to England or North Africa. They supported the allied invasion of Sicily, the Italian mainland, Salerno, on 9 September 1943 (when Italy surrendered); and on 22 January, they supported the Anzio landings in Italy.

The invasion of Normandy on the 6th of June 1944, opened up Europe to the Allied Forces. Off the beaches of Normandy, the American battleships the USS *Nevada*, the USS *Texas*, the USS *Arkansas* provided shore bombardment from 6,000 to 12,000 yards, as well as anti-aircraft protection for the Fleet. The Normandy landings were followed on the 25 June 1944 with additional landings in France at Cherbourg. It was off Cherbourg that the *Nevada*, in company with the *Texas* and *Arkansas*, received shore fire from German 88 guns. The *Nevada* provided support along the French coast to Marseilles.

USS New York *at sea. A Huge floating plateau of ice dwarfs the mighty battleship* New York *of the United States Navy in North Atlantic encounter. The* New York, *flagship of battleship division five of the fleet, is cruising with midshipmen of the 1st and rd class of the United States Naval Academy on board.*

Once the Allies had attained a secure hold on the mainland of Europe, American battleships worked their way to the Pacific Ocean. In June 1943, the USS *South Dakota* made a short visit to Atlantic waters but returned to the Pacific by the end of June 1943. The USS *Iowa* stood watch over the German battleship *Tirpitz* in Norway, and in November 1943, carried President Franklin D. Roosevelt to the Allied Conference in Teheran. By January 1944, the USS *Iowa* was in the Pacific providing escort cover for the aircraft carrier strikes against the Japanese outer, and later, inner home islands.

The end of World War II came with the Japanese surrender on 14 August 1945, just four months after the surrender in Europe on 7 May 1945. The battleships soon found themselves providing transportation back to America for thousands of troops. Most of the battleships at the end of the war were to be sold for scrap. Several, including the USS *New York*, the USS *Nevada*, the USS *Arkansas*, and the USS *Pennsylvania* were used in a series of atomic bomb tests at Bikini Island in the Pacific. The ships were sunk as a result of the bomb tests, or from supporting surface vessels after the tests. The *Nevada* and the *Pennsylvania*, even after the tests, refused to pass on easily and had to be deliberately sunk.

A number of battleships was fortunate and became military memorials. Individuals appreciating not only their tourist value, but their historical value and educational worth to future generations, kept them from the scrap pile. Today, the USS *Texas* (BB-35) is off the San Jacinto Battleground Park. The USS *North Carolina* (BB-55) sits in a channel just off Capre Fear River. The USS *Alabama* (BB-60) is off Jubilee Parkway (Interstate 10) by Mobile, and the USS *Arizona* (BB-39) rests at the sight of her sinking in Pearl Harbor, a national memorial since 1962. The USS *Massachusetts* (BB-59) is berthed at Fall River, MA and is a state shrine.

In the case of some battleships, where events prohibited the presentation of a complete battleship, artifacts have been pre-

The USS Arizonia Memorial at Pearl Harbor.

served. Artifacts have been obtained and are on display throughout the country for the USS *California* (BB-44), the USS *Maryland* (BB-46), the USS *Mississippi* (BB-41), the USS *Nevada* (BB-36), the USS *Oklahoma* (BB-37), the USS *Pennsylvania* (BB-38), the USS *Tennessee* (BB-43), the USS *West Virginia* (BB-48), the USS *Indiana* (BB-58), and the USS *South Dakota* (BB-57).

HERE WE GO AGAIN

No sooner had Americans taken off their shoes to enjoy the peace than the world became caught up in the "Cold War." On 25 June 1950, the United States of America found herself in a new war, facing a new enemy: North Korea, and later, Red China. The war began with a scramble for men and equipment. Ill-equipped and ill-trained Americans again found themselves on the short end of the stick.

The need for guns, big guns, accurate guns, led to the call for battleships. The USS *Iowa*, the USS *New Jersey*, the USS *Missouri*, and the USS *Wisconsin* went out to make believers of another generation of enemies. It was on the other side of the world, to most Americans, that the power of battleships was to be applied throughout 1951, 1952, and 1953. The "big boys" provided offshore fire support for Army and Marine units. The battleships, on rotation, were to supply walls of steel between our forces and the enemy from the Inchon landings to the evacuation at Hungnam Harbor. The signing of an Armistice on 27 July 1953 permitted the "big boys" to return home again.

And Again

For a time, this nation was to try to withdraw into itself, away from war and the threats of war. Unfortunately for us, but fortunately for the rest of the world, we did not pick up and leave the scene. Since World War II, this country has found itself involved in the political and war activities of South East Asia. In a series of events and political decisions, this country has been again at war - a sometimes-strange war that has left its mark on America.

However, whatever the politics, when needed for duty, the battleship was again to answer the call. The USS *New Jersey* got suited up again, and in September 1968, went back on the firing line, this time off the Vietnam coast. The USS *New Jersey* was again to demonstrate what she did best — blasting the hell out of the enemies' shore gun positions and troop facilities. The USS *New Jersey* manned with an all-volunteer crew was to be on the firing line for over 100 days. With the American evacuation of Vietnam in 1973, the USS *New Jersey* returned home, and was decommissioned in December 1969.

And Again

Following the Vietnam War, large-scale confrontations between nations degenerated into hit-and-run terrorist attacks throughout the world on Americans and their allies. In almost a throwback to 1812, our forces were called upon to take action in the Eastern Mediterranean. To support and beef-up our presence, the call again was for battleships to protect landings and to provide gun cover for our aircraft carriers forced to operate within the narrow seas surrounding Lebanon and Syria. The USS *New Jersey* was back in a familiar role. Following the *New Jersey*, the country recalled to duty the USS *Iowa*, the USS *Missouri*, and the USS *Wisconsin*.

Throughout the 1980s the battleship continued to be on the line for the United States. Today, the USS *New Jersey*, USS *Missouri,* USS *Wisconsin*, and the USS *Iowa* remain on active duty. The *New Jersey* and the Iowa are programmed to be off the active duty list in 1991.

With what seems like a back down of communist control in Eastern Europe, the money crunch for the military forces is with us again. There is a possibility of economics forcing a military system trade-off, and we may find this nation again without the services of our battleships.

Tomorrow

The reign of the battleship came to an end in the early 1990's when the final shots were fired during Desert Storm in the Persian Gulf War. The American Battleship lasted less than a century and fought in few ship to ship duels as its designers had wistfully envisioned. Instead, they served to defend the fast carrier forces against enemy aircraft, and releive embattled troops ashore who were slugging it out with dug in ground forces in the Pacific, Korea, and Vietnam.

In the end, the United States Navy built the finest and most durable of all battleships in the four ship Iowa class. All but three have become museum ships. The USS *Iowa* BB-61 was the last to feel the sea beneath her keel as she was towed from the east coast of the United States to her semi-permament mooring at the Suisun Bay Reserve Fleet in Northern California in April 2001. Doubtless, she too will become a museum ship in the Bay Area of San Francisco.

The most poigniont of the battleship memorials is that located at Pearl Harbor where the USS *Arizona* lies at the bottom of the harbor and symbolizes the beginning of the greatest war in human history (1941), and just yards away, the USS *Missouri*, on whose deck the surrender ceremony occurred that ended that same war in 1945. It was during that war that the USS *New York* and others like her made such valiant contributions to help ensure the continued safety and freedom of United States. If for no other reason, the value of the battleship in the arsenal of the American Navy was proven over and over again.

The great battleships that once roamed the oceans will likely never again be seen, however, what they acheived will never be forgotten.

In the final analysis, the battleships, the men who served in them, and the nation that employed them have all left their marks on history. Whatever the job, whatever the location, when called, the battleship answered, and no one ever had cause to doubt their worth, especially the enemy!

Manning the rail for F. D. R., 1939.

USS *NEW YORK* (BB-34) HISTORY
"THE OLD LADY OF THE SEA"

BY KERMIT BONNER

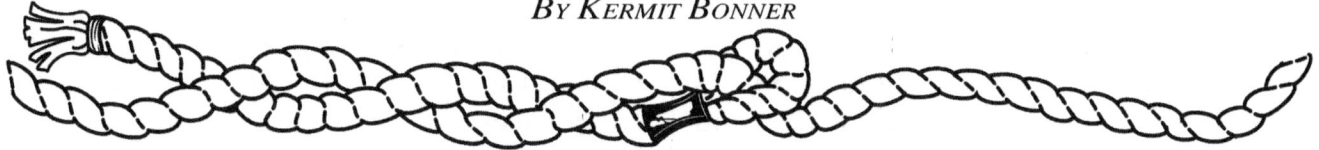

LABOR LAW BATTLESHIPS

Shortly after the turn of the century the labor movement in the U.S. was moving into high gear and in 1910, warship construction became subject to certain new restrictions. If a shipyard wanted to build a warship under contract to the U.S. government, it had to obey the new employee welfare and protection laws being enacted by the U.S. Congress. The June 24, 1910 act that authorized the funding for the construction of the battleships *New York* BB-34 and the *Texas* BB-35 specified the following conditions: build two first class battleships exclusive of armor and armament for less than $6 million each, and in accordance with the recent act that limited daily working hours for laborers on public works jobs. These were the first two major warships built pursuant to the new labor laws that restricted employers from requiring unlimited working hours per workweek. Although industrialists and manufacturers predicted economic ruin with this degree of latitude now accorded workers, both ships were built within specified time limits and within budget. Both also went on to long and illustrious careers. The USS *Texas* still exists as a naval memorial in *Texas*, a tribute to her builders. Her sister, the *New York* persisted until mid 1948 having survived two wars and two Atomic blasts. She was finally dispatched after an eight hour pounding by gunfire and aircraft bombs. The ship named in honor of the Empire State also proved her worth in war and was a tribute to her builders skill and dedication. This is her story.

THE *NEW YORK*: FIRST BATTLESHIP WITH THE FOURTEEN INCH GUN

The *New York* and her sister, *Texas* were the first U.S. battleships built with the new 14 inch/45 caliber gun as their main battery. They were also the first battleships in any of the world's navies to mount the 14 inch gun. This did not last long however, as battleship design and construction was among the most fluid of overall military armaments. The rapidly changing battleship was only rivaled by progress in aeronautical design. Before the *New York* and *Texas* slid down the ways, Great Britain and Germany had already begun work on ships with

USS New York *(BB-34) underway at high speed, 29 May 1915. (U.S. National Archives)*

larger caliber guns. The *New York* mounted ten 14 inch guns in five turrets that were sited in an A, B, Q, X and Y positions. At first, they had a maximum elevation of 15 degrees, but this was increased to 30 degrees just prior to the United State's entry into World War II. The increase in elevation was a common adjustment made to pre war battleships and improved their range dramatically. The *New York* and *Texas* were to be the last American battleships with a gun turret mounted amidships. All future designs would use either the four turret the A, B, X, and Y format or three turret A, B and Y format. The midships located battery was only one step up from the then obsolete wing mounted turrets, but was necessary to provide a sufficiently powerful broadside to compete with foreign variants. When the *New York* and *Texas* were designed, the U.S. Navy required at least twelve 12 inch guns be mounted for a competitive broadside, but the design did not provide for lengthening the ships to accommodate a six turret 12 inch battery. Consequently the battery caliber was increased to the new 14 inch/45 caliber thus only ten barrels would be required to throw the same weight as twelve 12 inch barrels. American battleships would never again employ the five turret format and all future designs would utilize a different arrangement with either four turrets or three turrets carrying two or three barrels. The next successive design after the *New York (Nevada* class) would use the four turret arrangement of 3 - 2 -2 - 3 fourteen inch barrels.

The *New York* class also mounted the single purpose casemate housed 5 inch/51 caliber gun to deal with destroyers and torpedo boats. Like their predecessors, the *Arkansas* and *Wyoming*, the casemate guns proved ineffective in any kind of a sea, yet the U.S. Navy was to hold on to this concept for at least two successive designs. It would not be until the *New Mexico* class would the Navy finally abandon the lower deck casemate gun. Aside from the difficulty experienced by gun crews in serving these guns, the guns had a short range and would probably not have been of any use against the quick and elusive destroyer. The *New York* was initially armed with sixteen 5 inch/51 caliber guns, eight to a side. In addition, as an afterthought during a later refit, this class was also armed with eight single 3 inch/50 caliber antiaircraft guns mounted four to a side. The initial antiaircraft defense was not in any way capable of defending the ship against aerial attack and especially not twenty five years later. Even the addition of 50 caliber machine guns did little to augment the pitiful antiaircraft defense. But, in 1915, the airplane was still a novelty and not considered to be anything more than an irritation in naval warfare. This same feeling was to persist for the next quarter century and would not be dispelled until the British success at Taranto in 1940 and of course, the Japanese victory at Pearl Harbor in December 1941. Harsh reality then set in, and the battleship would have to become a floating fortress against it's newest and most formidable nemesis, the aluminum and fabric airplane. All in all, the battleship diehards considered it unfair and almost unsporting that something as expensive, strong and solid as the battleship would be at the mercy of something as frail and economical as the airplane.

Incredibly, the *New York* class reverted to reciprocating machinery for its propul-

An excellent view of the aft half of the battleship New York *on July 26, 1919. Her decks are relatively uncluttered, and she has virtually no superstructure. At most, she is a hull with five large turrets and two cage masts. This would later change over the years as her AA battery was improved from wholly inadequate to impressive. The mushroom-like discs that dot her deck are ventilators.*

sion system as opposed to steam turbine drive which was coming into popularity in the European Navies. Even the *New York's* immediate predecessors, the *Wyoming* and *Arkansas* had been equipped with the turbine drive as was the grandfather of all modern battleships, HMS *Dreadnought*. There were valid reasons however. The reciprocating engineering plant was desired by contemporary naval engineers and American manufacturers had little real experience in building plants that met naval specifications. The reciprocating plant was considered more economical than the relatively untried turbine system especially at cruising speeds. Thus was important for a navy that might be called upon to fight a war a long way from home (e.g. near Japan), and spent much time cruising long distances in patrolling the Pacific. Only one additional American capital ship would be equipped with reciprocating machinery and that was the battleship *Oklahoma* of the *Nevada* class.

The propulsion plants installed aboard the *New York* and *Texas* consisted of two sets of four cylinder, triple expansion reciprocating steam engines both built by the Newport News Shipbuilding and Drydock Company. Fourteen coal fired Babcock and Wilcox boilers provided steam to two engines each connected to 142 foot long shafts turning one of the two 18 foot diameter three blade propellers. The fourteen boilers would eventually be replaced by six Bureau Express oil fired boilers. Each engine was rated at 14,050 shaft horsepower for a total of 28,100 shp. This was highly satisfactory and the ship was easily driven at a top speed of 21 knots due to the shape of the hull which had been designed for up to 32,000 shp. The engine rooms were more spacious than normal at over 1,500 square feet (60 feet x 26 feet) probably due to the designers anticipating both ships being re-engined with the more space consuming steam turbine system. With all of these seeming benefits, the *New York* and her sister were dated with coal fired boilers. This would change during her refit in 1926-1927 at the Norfolk Navy Yard, but from her commissioning on April 14, 1914 until her major refit 12 years later, her crew endured the filthiest job in the Navy - coaling.

The *New York* was not armored on the "all or nothing" concept as would be the follow on class, the *Nevada*. The *New York* was armored with carbon hardened belt armor above and below her waterline ranging from 12 to 9 inches thick. The armor plate consisted of eight foot steel sections riveted to the hull. The rest of the ship was protected in the same fashion as other battleships of the day. Bulkheads were 6 to 9 inches in thickness and the main deck was

Overhead of the ship taken in 1919 while she was steaming at 17 knots. Was taken from a kite balloon which increased visibility of the ship's spotters. Long barreled 5"ers and derrick top 3"ers are easily visible. (USN photo)

just under 4 inches in thickness. The turrets were armored with six inches on the sides, 12 inches rear, four inches on the roof and 12 inches on the face plates. The barbettes were 12 inches and the conning tower and tube, 12 inches. At the time that the *New York* was designed, it was expected that a capital ship would be faced primarily with medium and large caliber shell fire at a low angle of trajectory, if not a flat trajectory. The concept of plunging fire or aerial bombs was not yet accounted for in armor design and would not until successive generations of the "all or nothing" defense.

Compartments aboard the *New York* were situated around the engine rooms and main battery turret handling spaces and magazines. Propulsion and firepower was far more important than creature comfort. Senior and junior officers as well as commissioned warrant ranks occupied the forward part of the ship under the anchor handling area. The wardroom was directly under the main deck as was the officers lavatory facilities. When a heavy or even moderate sea was running, use of the officers head must have been exciting if not downright dangerous. This class of battleship was not renowned for it's seakeeping ability nor as stable ride. Interestingly the forward most compartment in the ship underneath the officers water closet or head was the storage area for general mess supplies and more specifically cigars and tobacco products. The early and middle twentieth century navy operated on fuel oil, tobacco and good coffee. Changes in military philosophy and improved health consciousness has done away with many of the staples of the early navy and unfortunately much of the lore and legend that gave this branch of the service it's mystique and romanticism. Navy coffee was always best when a pinch of salt was added to the pot, but now there are a hundred reasons why coffee, salt and of course tobacco are not healthy or heart smart. If these items are considered hazardous to one's health as the Navy approaches the 21st Century, dieticians would be appalled at the amount of fat, starch and protein contained in the average ship's meal of a half century ago.

The captain and admiral's quarters were located just behind the conning tower and the chief petty officers lived at the after end of the ship on deck level two. The crew occupied various areas on decks two and three from the stern forward to immediately behind barbette two. Many of the crew slept in the five inch gun casemate compartments in hammocks that were slung at night and stowed during the day. More senior petty officers had spring bunks aft that by wartime grew to four deep. Mattresses were less than 3 inches in thickness, but preferable to the standard hammock. The interior bulkheads of the ship was painted white and the floors covered in red-like asphalt tile. Psychologically, the dark reddish flooring was intended to reduce the level of fear of the common sailor when men were killed or wounded in battle and blood flowed freely. Fortunately, this never occurred on the *New York*.

The *New York* was equipped as a flagship from the outset as were most capital ships. She was normally manned by crew of 1314 men during peacetime which would swell to 1530 in war. In peacetime she was crowded, and in wartime the problem was far greater. Privacy was not possible for most men except the captain and certain senior officers. Getting along in crowded conditions and maintaining high morale was always a problem for any ship, but in most cases was overcome by cooperation and organization. In a ship like the *New York*, everything and everyone had a place, and only when something was out of order would disruption occur. Absolute organization and adhering to the rules was crucial. The *New York* was always considered a happy and taut ship.

The *New York* was 573 feet in length overall and had a 95 foot beam before the addition of torpedo bulges increased the maximum beam to 106 plus feet. She displaced 27,000 tons initially and 32,000 tons full load. Compared to the World War II *Iowa* class which displaced 45,000 tons and was nearly 900 foot in length, the *New York* was a small ship.

THE BATTLESHIP *NEW YORK* – IN TIME FOR WORLD WAR I

The *New York* was built by the New York Navy Yard, a government owned and operated shipyard. After congressional approval and funding had been granted, battleship number 34 had her keel laid on September 11, 1911. Fifteen months later she was launched on October 30, 1912. She was christened by Miss Elsie Calder, and for nearly 18 months, she was fitted out and prepared for acceptance and commissioning. She was commissioned on April 15, 1914, exactly two years before the first national income tax became effective. The *New York*'s first skipper was Thomas S. Rodgers, and she went to sea for further trials. Her shakedown period was cut short however, as she was sent to Vera Cruz in July 1914 as the flagship of Rear Admiral Frank Fletcher. Democracy was being threatened by the Huerta government, and the U.S. and it's new professor president, Woodrow Wilson was not about to stand for it. The Navy was dispatched to Vera Cruz to blockade the port from arms shipments that were on their way to the revolutionary government. The blockade was a success, but not before some furious street fighting in the city that resulted in the death of several Mexican revolutionaries. With a short time, democracy was restored and the *New York* was allowed to resume her shakedown and patrol routine along the Atlantic coast. This routine was interrupted periodically by the good will of her crew for those less fortunate ashore. The *New York* earned the nickname the "Christmas Ship" when she hosted a massive Christmas party and dinner for hundreds of New York City orphans. The crew suggested this and her captain in December 1915, Hugh Rodman heartily endorsed this idea. It was to become a tradition for this ship and many other to care for the needy whenever possible. This U.S. Navy tradition has continued for many decades. Ship's crews frequently volunteer to help others with money or assistance around the world. Ships are often the most immediately available sources of aid to areas that have suffered natural disasters, and the U.S. Navy never shirks it's humanitarian obligations. So it was with the battleship *New York*.

From the Vera Cruz incident until the U.S. entry in World War I, the *New York* spent her time in training and exercises off the Atlantic coast. When war was declared she sailed for Great Britain to reinforce the Grand Fleet in the North Sea. She was the flagship of Battleship Division 9 under the overall command of former *New York* skipper Hugh Rodman, now promoted to Rear Admiral. The *New York* arrived in the Royal Navy's northern outpost of Scapa Flow on December 7, 1917 prepared to join the Allies against Germany. It was bitterly cold in Northern Scotland, but wars do not usually occur in temperate climates. The *New York* was often sent on patrol and convoy duty and the presence of a modern American force of capital ships undoubtedly inhibited the Germans from breaking out of their coastal ports as they had at Jutland. The specter of another major fleet action where battleships belching black smoke pounded each other at long range was not again to happen in World War I. Her service in World War I did not result in any shots being fired in anger, yet she did witness several surface attacks on submarines that attempted to penetrate convoy defenses. Also during her deployment as part of the Allied fleet, she was visited by much of the British nobility including *King George V* and the *Prince of Wales* who would later abdicate his throne for the love of an American divorcee. The *New York* was of great interest to many who came to see what the "colonial rebels" considered a dreadnought. European dignitaries were not the only interested visitors. In early November 1918, Emperor Hirohito of Japan then a Crown Prince and Admiral of the Imperial Japanese Navy was welcomed aboard for an inspection. No doubt his interest was more than that of a foreign dignitary paying respect to another government.

Before going back home to the U.S., the *New York* was present at one of the most dramatic of all naval events, the surrender of the pride of the German Navy, the High Seas fleet. This event took place on November 21, 1918, in the Firth of Forth just days after the Armistice was signed. A few days later these magnificent ships would be scuttled by their disenchanted crews as a show of final defiance. For this they were imprisoned for a short period but in the spirit of peace eventually freed. The hatred and bitterness still existed and again boiled over some 20 years later.

The *New York* was called upon for one final chore before sailing for home, and that was to provide escort for President Wilson on his trans-Atlantic voyage to France to participate in the formation and signing of the Treaty of Versailles. This document was to end war on the European continent and pave the way for lasting peace and ultimately the League of Nations. A noble gesture that the world was too immature to take advantage of at that time.

This done, the four year old battleship arrived back in the U.S. to take up training and patrol duties again. Her travels took her to the Caribbean along with the rest of the fleet. In late 1919 she sailed for the Pacific and joined the newly formed Pacific Fleet. She would be a part of this fleet until the mid 1930's when she would then return to the cold northern waters of the Atlantic. She did make periodic sojourns to the other side of the U.S. and on one such trip, remained at the Norfolk Navy Yard for a complete refit.

THE *NEW YORK* IS SPARED: THE TREATY HATCHET AND GETS A NEW LEASE ON LIFE

The *New York* was over a decade old when she entered the Norfolk Navy Yard for a major refit. By other standards, she was obsolete compared to other battleships in the U.S. Navy's capital ship inventory and at an obvious disadvantage when contrasted with like ships in the world's major navies. She was a coal burner and her secondary battery was located virtually at sea level in an ineffective broadside arrangement. Her cage masts also identified her as behind the times and she was much slower at 21 knots than many of her potential opponents. Other ships of her genre were being selected for demilitarization or even scrapping. The *Wyoming* would become a gunnery training ship and the *Utah* was consigned to target duty in 1931. The *Utah*'s sister, the *Florida* was scrapped outright in 1931 as all of the pre-dreadnoughts had been in the 1920's. What was to become of the *New York* and her sister, the *Texas*? Fortunately, both were selected for a massive degree of modernization and refitting. Most of the rest of the fleet's more contemporary battleships would also be modernized in future years as would most of the capital ships in all of the major navies in the world. This was provided for under the provisions of the Naval Arms Limitation Treaties agreed to in 1922 and 1930. The *New York* and *Texas* were selected for upgrading and overall improvement. The *New York* would be refitted at the Norfolk Navy Yard during 1926 and 1927.

The *New York* was updated on four separate occasions during her 34 year ca-

The New York as she appeared in 1921. She has successfully weathered World War I, and is now part of the U.S. Fleet. She and her sister, the Texas, were the last battleships to be armed wtih five center line turrets. Future battleships would either have three or four turrets.

reer. Before entering the Norfolk Navy Yard she had been altered in 1919 when she landed five of her 5 inch/51 caliber secondary guns and additional 3 inch/50 caliber anti-aircraft guns were added. This was minor compared to the job that was to be done in Norfolk.

The 14 coal burning boilers were converted to six Bureau Express oil burning boilers and the twin funnels were trunked into one just aft of the forward superstructure. This was a major achievement and set very well with a crew tired of the filth and backbreaking work of periodic coaling. Tripods were also fitted in place of the obsolete lattice masts. Atop the massive forward tripod a control tower which looked much like a henhouse was installed, and the *New York* and sister *Texas* began to bear a resemblance to the rest of the battleships in the fleet. Both also had a truss like tower built amidships that contained additional fire control as somewhat of a back up to the system atop the fore mast. This was redundancy to the extreme, but it was a naval requirement of officers fearful of not having sufficient fire control backup. Fortunately, it did not interfere with the new catapult atop "Q" turret. A second catapult was fitted on the top of "Q" turret and cranes were installed on either side of the funnel for boat and aircraft handling. Some deck protection was added, and her beam widened to 106 feet with addition of anti-torpedo bulges along the water line. Unfortunately, there was heavy price to pay for the anti-torpedo bulges. The ship, never a really excellent sea boat, became almost unstable at lower speeds, particularly in swells or quartering seas. Anchoring in the open sea without the protection of a natural or manmade breakwater also made her roll heavily. The tendency to stiffness made it ever so much more difficult to maintain an adequate level of gunfire accuracy in certain conditions, a problem for a battleship engaged in shore bombardment.

The *New York* like sister *Texas* were the beneficiaries of the Washington Naval Treaty provision that allowed up to 3,000 tons to be added to existing capital ships for defense against aerial and submerged threats. This plus other obvious improvements rendered the *New York* a relatively modern battleship when she emerged from the yard in 1927.

The *New York* would be modernized two more times and they were in 1940-41 when her main battery elevation was increased from 15 degrees to 30 degrees, and later during World War II. Experience gained in the early years of the war mandated that all ships be made capable of defending themselves against aircraft. The *New York* had the balance of her secondary battery deck guns removed and her anti-aircraft battery was increased to ten 3 inch/50 caliber guns, twenty four 40mm and thirty six 20mm guns. RDF and improved fire control were also added to augment her AA defenses. All of this eventually increased her displacement to 29,340 tons or 34,000 tons full load.

The battleship was part of the Pacific Fleet until 1937 when she was selected to carry President Roosevelt's personal representative, Admiral Hugh Rodman to En-

USS New York anchored in Hampton Roads, Virginia, 17 October 1929. (USN photo)

gland for the coronation of King George VI. For the next several years, the New York would confine her activities to the Atlantic, and act primarily as a training ship for midshipmen and newly enlisted sailors. She was also selected to test radar in 1939, only the second ship after the destroyer Leary. She was equipped with the new and improved version that the naval electronics laboratory had been perfecting over the past decade. The set installed aboard the old battleship was not as sophisticated as that commonly used in World War II and beyond, but it was great step forward.

Off North Africa on 10 November 1942, just after the Battle of Casablanca. (USN photo)

The New York was a suitable test platform for radar as she was available and had adequate space aboard to accommodate the rather bulky radar installations characteristic of the early days. The tests were highly satisfactory and improved versions were introduced to other fleet units as quickly as was practical. All of the light cruisers of the Brooklyn/St. Louis class had radar and the battleship West Virginia had the trademark "bedspring mattress" antenna when she was sunk on December 7, 1941. It was not until the war was in it's second year that radar was common, and even then, many commanding officers did not trust it or understand it's potential. In any event, the first successful use of radar was on a battleship that had been judged overage in 1934, but overage or not, was destined for sterling service in World War II.

World War II and the New York

The New York was ordered to safeguard the sea lanes in the north Atlantic as part of the "Neutrality Patrol". When war broke out on the European continent in September 1939, it was just a matter of time before the U.S. would be a full fledged participant. For the next 27 months the New York and the rest of the Atlantic Squadron (later the Atlantic Fleet) became incrementally involved in the sea war which unfolded just off the east coast of isolationist America. American destroyers were protecting Allied convoys on their way to Great Britain, and suffering in the bargain. The destroyers Kearny and Reuben James were hit by U-boat torpedoes and the "short of war" approach quickly became total war. The New York and other battleships like sister Texas and the Arkansas banded together to shepherd supply ships, and in July 1941, the Empire State battlewagon protected ships carrying American troops to Iceland. Duty in northern waters was harsh for sailors and further complicated by numerous submarine contacts, attacks and counter attacks. And, this was just the dawn of the new war at sea.

The peaceful invasion of Iceland by the Americans was one of the most important events of Allied military strategy prior to the official entry of the U.S. in the second world war. The Icelandic government was concerned about the possibility of the 15,000 British Empire troops which were garrisoning their homeland being withdrawn for other more pressing battle commitments. In that event, a political vacuum might be filled by Axis troops and then a knife would be pointed toward North America. Then convoys that were none too safe as things were, would be at the complete mercy of the German Navy. Enter the U.S. Navy. The U.S. provided a ground force protected by ships like the *New York* and *Texas* as well as 21 other destroyers, cruisers and battleships. They replaced the Empire troops who were quickly deployed in more critical areas. Without ships like the *New York*, this maneuver would have been impossible. Saving her from the "scrap crazed" politicians of the 1920's treaty generation proved to be an excellent decision.

The attack on Pearl Harbor on December 7, 1941 and the formal declaration of war on the Axis powers in the following days caught the now veteran battlewagon in the Norfolk Navy Yard. She was going through her third refit which was to increase her main battery elevation and augment her still inadequate AA defense. The refit was accelerated and she was back at sea convoying cargo and troop ships to Iceland and Scotland within weeks.

Her first major operation was as a unit in *Operation Torch*, the November 1942 invasion of North Africa. It was the second amphibious invasion staged by the U.S. Navy and the largest to date. The invasion of Guadalcanal just four months before had been the first attempt made by ground troops supported by the navy in attacking enemy defended shore positions.

The attack on Guadalcanal proved to be a relative success but only by the grace of God and fortune. There was little initial opposition to the landings so ground troops were in place before massive Japanese retaliation. But, there were many mistakes including poor planning, inadequate naval gunfire support and logistics and supply end in a nightmare. Fortune smiled on the Allies however, and they learned from their mistakes. The landings in North Africa benefitted from lessons learned on the other side of the world, but there was a new obstacles to overcome. For one thing, it was unclear as to whether the Vichy French army and navy, would resist, and if so, to what degree. They invasion force would soon find out.

The *New York* was ordered to provide bombardment and call fire support for the Southern Attack Group which was to attack Safi beginning on the morning of November 8, 1942. The light cruiser *Philadelphia* (flagship of Rear Admiral Lyle Davidson) and six destroyers joined the *New York* and together they mounted the attack on Safi Harbor. The *New York* was also to provide gunfire support for the destroyers *Bernadou* and *Cole* which had been detailed to enter the harbor and deliver two specially trained companies of the 47th Infantry to seize the port. Also embarked were trained naval personnel designated to assume control and begin operating port facilities. Having a fully operational port would facilitate ground operations so this task was vital. The two destroyers were ancient World War I designed four pipers that had been modified to a fast troop transport role. Their masts were removed and the superstructure's reduced in size to minimize their silhouette. This proved to be the most valuable modification of all, as the French defenders later commented that they had looked in vain for masts and by the time they recognized the destroyers, it was too late. However, neither of these ships and their brave crews could withstand the pounding of a well handled shore battery, and that is what they came up against. As they steamed into the harbor entrance with no pilot and an out of date chart, they were fired upon by a 75mm battery, but their main battery silenced this threat. They were approached and challenged by a converted Vichy tug, the *Alphonse Delanade*, but she was quickly dispatched by well handled destroyer guns. Next it was the turn of small arms and heavy machine guns all around the harbor which converged on the speeding converted troop transports. This dealt with, it looked as if the assault force was home free. It was at this juncture that the largest shore battery at Point De La Tour (four 130mm heavy caliber naval guns) opened up on the destroyers. The ships were no match for this threat. Enter the *New York* and *Philadelphia*. Both opened fire at the offending battery

Pitching into heavy seas while en route from Casablanca on convoy escort duty, March 1943. View looks forward from her foremast. Note her twin 14"/45 gun turrets and water flowing over main deck. (USN photo)

and within a few salvoes, the battery was silenced. The dreaded "Batterie Railleuse" could have ended the assault as quickly as it had begun, but it was no match for the *New York*. It was later learned that one of her 14 inch salvoes had struck the base of the battery which was located on a cliff and the shells had ricocheted into the observation slits destroying the range finder and killing the battery commander. For all intents and purposes, the battery was out of commission and no longer a menace to the landing force. Later, at 0700 the battery opened up on the invaders but only under manual fire control. Earlier work by the *New York* had rendered the battery incapable of accuracy and it was unable to hit either the *New York* or *Philadelphia*. Aircraft from the escort carrier Santee arrived and acted as gunfire spotters and within minutes the battery was smothered by machine gun like 6 inch gunfire from the *Philadelphia*. The *New York* remained on station until it was determined that Safi was in Allied hands and she could be released to help out at the central sector of the invasion at the Fedala landing site.

The Center Group (fire support team) which included the cruisers *Brooklyn* and *Augusta* was charged with silencing the batteries protecting the port of Fedala and insuring that units of the French navy based at Casablanca did not interfere with the landings. Both ships with their accompanying destroyers had their hands full as did the new battleship *Massachusetts* which had to immobilize the modern French battleship Jean Bart. The Jean Bart did open fire on the invaders and French cruisers and destroyers sortied from Casablanca on several occasions to do battle with the *Brooklyn*, *Augusta* and other Allied ships. The French fleet was systemically destroyed in detail and the Jean Bart was damaged to the point of being unable to return fire. The *New York* had been called from her station to the south to assist, but by the time she was in position, the issue had been settled.

Operation Torch was a success and the *New York* was there to help insure victory. It was unfortunate that so many French sailors and soldiers were forced to die on the side of the Axis, but their leaders had chosen the wrong viewpoint. It was also a shame that the cream of the French cruiser/destroyer force was annihilated, but it proved that the U.S. Navy was capable of victory at sea. It was strange however to fight an enemy who before was a friend and after defeat would again be an ally.

When the beaches were secure the *New York* was ordered back to escort duty and accompanied two convoys from the U.S. to Casablanca over the next few months. After a short overhaul period the old battleship became a main battery and escort training center for the Navy, Coast Guard and personnel from various Allied navies. From July 1943 through June 1944 she was an effective training platform for 14 inch/45 caliber gun crews and also for close in weapons. Most escort vessels coming out of American shipyards used the 3 inch/50 caliber gun and the 20mm and 40mm weapons. As the *New York* fairly bristled with these guns, she was a perfect ship for training new gunners and gunnery officers. In the year that she was in this program over 11,000 men and 750 officers participated in the training. Another battleship, the *Wyoming* was used for 5 inch/38 gun training and 20mm/40mm gun training. These old war horses has much value, even if they were not constantly on the firing line.

After her assignment as a gunnery training ship was completed, the *New York* was seconded to the Naval Academy to make three midshipman cruises from Annapolis, Maryland to Trinidad, British West Indies. Over 1,800 "middies" learned from practical experience aboard the old battleship, but in the late autumn of 1944, it was time for her to return to more serious and dangerous work. Throughout December 1944 and into January 1945, she carried out refresher training off the Southern California coast. On January 12, 1945, she rejoined the fighting navy which was on it;s way to the climax of the war in the Pacific. It would be the last hurrah for the old battlewagon.

Iwo Jima, Okinawa and the Last Japanese Gasp

In the early days of 1945, victory was pretty much taken for granted. It was now just a matter of time before the almost defeated Axis Powers would finally succumb to the continuous Allied destruction of their military and civilian resources. To western thinking, defeating an enemy meant subverting his will to win. Unfortunately, the Imperial Japanese military machine was not bound by occidental rules of engagement and would doggedly resist to the point of complete annihilation. The battle for Iwo Jima was forecast of what might come as the U.S. Navy moved closer to the Japanese home islands. The next objective, Okinawa further became a sounding board for what would happen should the Allies attempt a landing on Kyushu, the main Japanese home island. These were not battles but rather contests between men who wanted to live and those who sought to die by killing them. It was a hideous and frightening look into the future. It could be summed up in one word - Kamikaze.

The capture and development of Iwo Jima into a fighter plane base and emergency facility for bombers was a necessary step for the strategic bombing of the Japanese homeland. Pilots needed a base near their target so that they could nurse their damaged B-29's into friendly skies at the earliest possible opportunity. It would also provide a base for some of the Army Air Force's long legged escort fighters such as the P-51 Mustang. Iwo Jima was also a milestone in the island hopping campaign. Next stop, Japan itself. The job of softening up it's formidable defenses fell to the old reliable's - battleships *Idaho*, *Tennessee*, *Nevada*, *Texas*, *Arkansas*, and of course, the *New York*.

Unfortunately, the *New York* lost a blade off of her port screw and was forced to seek repair just before the invasion began. She was in time however for the pre-invasion bombardment which began on February 16, 1945. This continued for three days. The old battleship was constantly firing at one target or another and expended 6,417 rounds of ammunition. She fired 1,037 fourteen inch shells alone and laid claim to the most spectacular secondary explosion in the campaign when one of her main battery shells hit the enemy's primary ammunition dump.

Still limping as the result of temporary repairs to the port propeller, she went on to a forward repair base at Manus for permanent restoration. This completed, she rejoined Task Force 54, the old reliable's and all steamed toward Okinawa. This fire support team had been further augmented by the arrival of the *Maryland*, *Colorado* and *West Virginia*. With the notable exception of the *Arizona* and *Oklahoma*, almost all of the pre-war battleships were present for the finale of the Pacific War. Beginning on March 27, 1945, the *New York* provided 76 continuous days of unremitting gunfire support to ground forces. She expended 4,159 rounds of fourteen inch ammunition, and a further 7,001 five inch. Her gun barrels were worn out by the time she was detached on June 11.

She was also subjected to a number of suicide plane attacks and was slightly damaged by one on April 14, 1945. She was at Pearl Harbor having her guns relined and being prepared for the invasion of Japan when the war ended on August 15, 1945. She was now 34 years old, and obsolete by all standards. Her active military service was at an end. She made a "magic carpet" cruise with veterans from the Pacific and was greeted by singer Dinah Shore in San Pedro on September 5, 1945.

The war was over, and the Japanese had been thoroughly defeated. It had been a long and arduous journey for millions of men and women as well as thousands of ships. The old battleships were no longer of any military value as they had been eclipsed by the new capital ship, the carrier. All that was left was one of three choices; preservation as a memorial, scrapping or use as a target.

The *New York* was selected for option number three - target practice.

OPERATION CROSSROADS AND THE END

The *New York* along with over 70 plus other ships was selected for the twin atomic bomb tests at Bikini Atoll in July 1946. She survived both blasts, much to the credit of her builders. The anti-Navy faction that predicted that the nuclear age spelled the end of navies was unnerved to see ships like the *New York* survive, virtually intact and still ready for action.

She was then towed to Pearl Harbor and the effects of the atomic bomb blasts were studied through mid 1948. On July 6, 1948, she was towed out to sea and two days later subjected to eight hours of target practise by modern aircraft and ships. Finally she succumbed and sank. The "Old Lady of the Sea" was gone and with her one of the last vestiges of an age gone by, an age when brave men made the difference rather than computer capacity.

Bombarding Japanese defenses on Iwo Jima, 16 February 1945. She has just fired the left-hand 14"/45 gun of Number Four turret. View looks aft, on the starboard side. (USN photo)

Bibliography

Baldwin, Hanson W., Battles Won and Lost (New York, 1966).

Bonner, Kermit, Final Voyages, (Turner Publishing Company, Paducah, KY 1999).

Bowditch, Nathaniel, L.L.D., American Practical Navigator (Washington, 1962).

Breyer, Siegfried, Battleships and Battle Cruisers, 1905-1907 (New York, 1973).

Cates, Jr. Clifton, War History of The U.S.S. Pennsylvania (BB38), published by the ship's welfare fund.

Ewing, Steve, Memories and Memorials, (Montana, 1986).

Fuller, J. F. C., A Military History of the Western World, Volume 3, (New York, 1956).

Howarth, David, The Dreadnoughts, (Alexandria, 1979).

Hoyle, Martha Byrd, A World in Flames, (New York, 1970).

Knight, Austin M. Late R.A. U.S.N., Modern Seamanship
(New York, 1953).

Loft, Arnold S., U.S.N. (Ret) and Sumyall, Robert F., HTC.

USNR, U.S.S. North Carolina (BB55), (Annapolis, 1973).

Morison, Samuel Eliot, The Liberation of the Philippines.

Luzon, Mindanao, the Visayas. 1944-1945, (Boston, 1953).

Potter, E.B., The Illustrated History of the United States Navy
(New York City, 1971).

Salmaggi, Cesare, and Pallavisini, Alfredo, 2194 Days of War,
(New York, 1977).

Smith, Jr. Myron J., Keystone Battleship, U.S.S. Pennsylvania,
(BB38), Charleston, 1983).

Swaney, Edwin S., Operation Crossroads, (Montezuma, 1986).

Turner Publishing Company, American Battleships, (Paducah, KY 1990)

United States Navy Department, Dictionary of American Naval Fighting Ships, Vol. I., (Washington, 1959).

United States Navy Department, Dictionary of American Naval Fighting Ships, Vol. V., (Washington, 1979).

H. R. "Shorty" Reynold's last voyage, 1946.

USS *New York* (BB-34)
"The Old Lady of the Fleet"
OUR CENTURY'S "OLD IRONSIDES"
Navy Day Celebration - 27 Oct 1945 -
New York City

"Something to shoot at!" She did it. A statistical summary of the record of the USS *New York* shows the following:

OPERATIONS:
1088 days with the Atlantic Fleet (December 1941-November 1944)
North African Landings (Safi)
2 Convoy Trips to Iceland
2 Convoy Trips to Scotland
2 Convoy Trips to Casablanca
Training Duty in the Caribbean Sea and Chesapeake Bay
276 Days with the Pacific Fleet
Assault on Iwo Jima
Assault and Occupation of Okinawa Shima

DAMAGE SUSTAINED AND PERSONNEL CASUALTIES:

On 14 April 1945, a Japanese suicide plane attacked the *New York* off Okinawa, demolishing one *New York* spotting plane on the catapult and crashing some 50 yards from the ship. The *New York* received only superficial damage.

Two men were slightly wounded in action during the suicide plane attack of April 1945.

AMMUNITION EXPENDED BY OPERATIONS:

		Rounds	Pounds
NORTH AFRICAN LANDINGS			
	14"/45 (bombardment)	60	76,500
IWO JIMA			
	14"/45 (bombardment)	1,037	1,322,175
	5"/51 (bombardment)	719	35,950
	3"/50 (bombardment)	526	7,101
	40mm (bombardment)	4,135	
		6,417	1,365,226
OKINAWA SHIMA			
	14"/45 (bombardment)	4,159	5,302,725
	5"/51 (bombardment)	7,001	350,050
	3"/50 (bombardment)	183	2,471
	3"/50 (bombardment)	62	837
	40mm (bomb. and AA)	2,731	
	20mm (anti-aircraft)	2,481	
	30 cal. (strafing)	30,000	
	40mm (bombardment)	1,170	
	40mm (anti-aircraft)	1,561	
	20mm (anti-aircraft)	2,481	
	30 cal. (strafing)	30,000	
		46,617	5,656,083

AMMUNITION EXPENDED BY CALIBER
BOMBARDMENT:

14"/45	5,256
5"/51	7,720
3"/50	709
40mm	5,305
	18,990

ANTI-AIRCRAFT:

3"/50	62
40mm	1,561
20mm	2,481
	4,104

STRAFING:

	30 cal.	30,000
Total Rounds All Types	53,094	

WEIGHT OF AMMUNITION EXPENDED BY CALIBER

	Pounds	Tons
14"/45	6,701,400	3,350.7
5"/51	386,000	193.0
3"/50	10,409	5.2
	7,097,809	3,548.9

SHIP'S OPERATIONS IN GENERAL:
  Total miles steamed during the war, 123,867
  Total hours underway during the war, 9,942.7—the equivalent of 414 days
  Total fuel oil consumption during the war, 22,367,996 gallons

USS New York *BB34 1946 - Last Trip*

CHRONOLOGY OF USS *NEW YORK* FEBRUARY 1942-OCTOBER 1945

This is a brief diary of Phillip R. Carter who went aboard the USS *New York* in February 1942 and stayed aboard until the end of hostilities of Germany and the surrender of Japan.

He was told not to keep a diary, but did keep the sailing dates and relates to some of the most important events while he was aboard.

He left New Orleans December 27, 1941, destination Norfolk, on a troop train with 200 other recruits all determined to even the score with the Axis powers.

The recruits consisted of mixed blood lines: the Arcadian French from the bayous, the Atchafalaya Basin, Vieuxcarre, and the New Orleans French Quarter, who spoke a French peppered with elements of English, German and Spanish. Then there were Bilox fishermen from the Gulf Coast and farmers from inland, fresh from behind the plow. They were soon assimilated with Brooklynites, Westerners and Northerners into a formidable fighting force.

After a brief training period at Norfolk, most of his platoon was assigned to the USS *New York* at dock at Portsmouth; others were assigned to various ships and stations; some were assigned to tankers and other ships. A few had already lost their lives due to the intense German submarine activity off the Atlantic seaboard; organized defense against the U-boats was not yet effective and many merchant and naval vessels were lost.

The following sailing dates are accurate to the best of his knowledge as well as some important events that took place:

Departed	Arrived
Norfolk, 2-15-42	New York, 2-16-42
New York, 2-16-42	Nova Scotia, 2-21-42
Nova Scotia, 2-21-42	Iceland, 3-2-42

This on the job training was bewildering to an apprentice seaman. My first job was lookout in secondary forward (crow's nest). To get there in the rough icy North Atlantic weather, I donned foul weather gear and climbed the icy rungs to my station while the ship rolled near 40 degrees.

These trips to Iceland were necessary to safeguard the large convoys of troop and cargo ships sailing on their first leg to the British Isles from surface raiders. The British Navy convoyed them from Iceland to their destination.

Departed	Arrived
Iceland, 3-14-42	Norfolk, 3-27-42
Norfolk, 4-24-42	New York, 4-2542
New York, 4-30-42	Nova Scotia, 5-2-42
Nova Scotia, 5-3-42	Newfoundland, 5-5-42
Newfoundland, 5-5-42	Iceland, 5-10-42
Iceland, 5-12-42	New York, 5-20-42
New York, 5-21-42	Nova Scotia, 6-2-42
Nova Scotia, 6-3-42	Scotland, 6-10-42

There were few incidents on these convoy trips because we were far to the north where the icy North Atlantic kept the U-boats at bay. Some ships broke down or could not keep up. As part of a relief crew on a 3" 50 one night, we witnessed a blinding flash on our starboard quarter and later found out the DD USS *Ingram* had collided with a tanker and had blown up with only 11 survivors. Then there was an incident where a green ensign gave the wrong order at the wheel, and the battleship got loose in the midst of the convoy. The Old Lady broke down on several occasions; generally the USS *Brooklyn* stood by.

The entrance into Scotland was a welcomed relief. The little farms along the banks of Firth of Fourth of Clyde were colorful, like grandmother's quilt. We anchored at Grennock; there were many bombed buildings and sunken vessels all around. We were given liberty in Grennock. Chaplain escorted us to Edinburgh on a little English train.

Departed	Arrived
Scotland, 6-16-42	New York, 6-26-42
New York, 6-29-42	Norfolk, 6-30-42

Every time the ship arrived at Norfolk, Portsmouth was waiting to install new equipment in order to upgrade the obsolete ship. 1.1s were replaced with 40mm's and 20mm's installed, which bristled along the deck. Cafeteria feeding was implemented instead of the serving by mess cooks carrying tureens from the galley and setting up in the living compartments. Improvements were made to the tripod masts; new electronic equipment was installed.

Departed	Arrived
Norfolk, 8-12-42	New York, 8-13-42
New York, ??	Nova Scotia, ??
Nova Scotia, 8-22-42	Scotland, 8-31-42
Scotland, 9-5-42	Norfolk, 9-15-42
Norfolk, 10-23-42	Safi, 11-8-42
Safi, 11-9-42	Casablanca, 11-11-42
Fedela, 11-14-42	Norfolk, 11-23-42

At Safi, Morocco, on November 8, the *New York* silenced the French battery Railleuse, her first shots in anger from both World Wars.

Chaplain Cummins recalled the ship's luck held at Safi when an enemy shell struck just below our 5-inch just as it was fired. The concussion floored the crew, but did little damage.

The ship almost turned over in a ground swell at Safi. A 14" shell injured my arm so badly I was put in sick bay. The ship then sailed to Casablanca to silence the French battleship *Jean Bart*; the *Jean Bart* being contained by the time we got there. While there, U-boats made a sneak attack past our destroyer screen two nights straight, firing torpedoes across the bow and stern of the Old Lady, hitting cargo ships both times. The decision was made then to slip the anchor chain and sail back to New York, leaving our prize crew stranded. They later joined the ship at another port.

Liberty at Casablanca. The Sultan of Morocco visited the ship on or about the third trip.

Departed	Arrived
Norfolk, 11-24-42	New York, Nov. 25-42
New York, 12-12-42	Casablanca, 12-24-42
Casablanca, 12-29-42	Norfolk, 1-12-43
Norfolk, 2-26-43	New York, 2-27-43

USS New York *scouting plane after being struck by a kamikaze April 14, 1945 at Okinawa.*

New York, 3-5-43	Casablanca, 3-18-43
Casablanca, 3-25-43	New York, 4-5-43
New York, 5-1-43	Portland, ME, 5-2-43
Portland, ME, 7-27-43	Norfolk, 8-2-43

As the new ships came off the ways, the *New York* was not needed as badly, so the crew enjoyed a couple months of badly needed rest in the beautiful island-studded waters of Casco Bay. I caught a lot of shore patrol duty, riding the trains between Portland and Boston.

Then back to Norfolk where the *Old Lady* was used for training DD officers and men in gunnery and seamanship. This school lasted one year, one month and 11 days off Hampton roads.

I had my day on one of these 14" gunnery runs on a tow target. Daniel Wellock, a pointer, (from Akron, OH), had power failure on his electric hydraulic Sperry Rand engine that elevated the left gun. I was pointer on the right gun and had to interlock the two guns together on the same mills; this gave me control of both. The sea was rough and I wrestled with the local control scope as did the trainer, until we were on target. One salvo was over, one under, one demolished the target at 23,000 yards. Not bad shooting for a rolling ship!

The monotony of Gunnery School had lowered morale, and mass requests for trans-

Five 20 MM guns on starboard 1/4 deck.

fers were put in. But finally we got a change of scene; the ship departed for Annapolis where we began midshipmen cruises.

Departed	**Arrived**
Norfolk, 6-13-44	Trinidad, BWI, 6-19-44
Trinidad, BWI, 6-30-44	Norfolk, 7-6-44
Norfolk, 7-11-44	Trinidad, 7-18-44
Trinidad, 8-9-44	Norfolk, 8-16-44
Norfolk, 11-21-44	Panama, 11-27-44
Panama, 11-27-44	Long Beach, 12-9-44

Foul weather gear was issued at Norfolk leading us to believe we were going north until we arrived at Panama. Tuscaloosa lost observation plane in route. After leaving Panama and entering the Pacific, the ship broke down as she had done so often in the North Atlantic. We were dead in the water for eight hours. I hardly blame the escorts from wanting to leave us.

Departed	**Arrived**
Long Beach, CA, 12-11-44	
	Frisco Islands, 12-12-44

Intense gunnery practice, so had the idea that we were going to be expendable in the Pacific fighting the Japanese who were still going strong with their kamikazes and sinking a lot of ships.

Departed	**Arrived**
Long Beach, CA, 12-11-44	
	Hawaiian Islands, 1-19-45

Smooth sailing; intense gunnery practice en route. Blew whistles as we passed sunken ships in harbor at Pearl.

Departed	**Arrived**
Pearl Harbor, 1-27-45	Eniwetok, 2-5-45
Eniwetok, 2-7-45	Saipan, 2-11-45

Lost blade off screw en route to Eniwetok; slowed speed to almost half. The convoy left us—lonely out there. James Lilley of Coden, AL, said that it was a near miss with a torpedo that cost us the blade. Lucky, lucky! Bathed in the Pacific first time at Eniwetok. Saipan was home of B-29 bomber base. Any land was a beautiful sight.

Departed	**Arrived**
Saipan, 2-13-45	Iwo Jima, 2-16-45

We were told that we could expect to receive heavy casualties at Iwo Jima, this little island 600 miles from Japan.

Departed	**Arrived**
Iwo Jima, 2-19-45	Ulithi, 2-21-45

Very successful shooting at Iwo, destroyed many gun emplacements. Took casualties from demolition crew aboard; three died en route; sea burial. Wounded were put ashore at Ulithi. Continued on to Manus to floating dry dock for a new blade. There seemed to be no end to the length and width of the Pacific; I thought I'd go stare crazy if I didn't see land soon.

On the way to Ulithi, I was relief gun captain on 3" 50 when the Bridge ordered me to shoot down a large metallic balloon that was clearly visible. The director didn't work, neither was there a range given. After the second call from the Bridge, I didn't hesitate but invented my own range and elevation and cut loose with 11 rounds. Then the weather officer inquired, "Why are you trying to shoot down Venus?"

Departed	Arrived
Ulithi, 2-22-45	Manus, 2-28-45

Put in floating dry dock but was kicked out when Philadelphia Naval Shipyards sent wrong pitched blade. They finally fixed us up. A fire controlman was killed after a LCVPs landing ramp fell on him during a beer party on one of the many little islands.

Departed	Arrived
Manus, 3-19-45	Ulithi, 3-22-45

Seemed we were flying at 15 knots after being restricted to half speed; re-armed at Ulithi.

Departed	Arrived
Ulithi, 3-23-45	Okinawa, 3-27-45

After a brief stop in the Philippines, we proceeded to Okinawa in the Ryukyus chain. It was the front door to Japan—taking it would mean much toward winning the war.

It would take a book to describe the *New York's* action at Okinawa. The softening up operations began three days before D-Day, April 1. I was rudely awakened on D-Day by a near miss of a 500-lb bomb. Then the action settled down to staying on station for 76 straight days—working for the Army and Marines. (You tell us where to put it and we'll oblige.) After expending our ammunition, the ship would retire to Kerama Rhetto, a horseshoe island about 18 miles off the coast, to re-arm, then back on station. The Japanese threw everything they had at us, including one suicide plane, wrecking one of our observation planes. The battle of Okinawa was fierce, some 200 air raids, boats with torpedoes tied to their bows, shell fire, buzz bombs and human bombs. (Ernest Pyle killed by sniper at Ie Shima; President Roosevelt died.) What a blessed relief as the fighting was confined to one end of the island. We were detached from duty here. Message from Vice Admiral Hill: "Your departure would bring comfort to a lot of Japanese were they alive to know of it."

Departed	Arrived
Okinawa, 6-11-45	Leyte, 6-14-45
Philippines, 6-17-45	Pearl Harbor, 7-1-45
Pearl Harbor, 9-2-45	San Pedro, 9-9-45

When we arrived at Pearl, new 14" guns were awaiting us on the dock; we had shot the liners out of the old ones. This was not comforting to us as we knew there was a long road to travel yet. But to everyone's surprise the Japanese surrendered aboard the USS *Missouri* Sept. 1, 1945. The ship took on 200 high-point men at Pearl and arrived at San Pedro to a hero's welcome. Movie stars roamed the ship at will, and even the Hollywood Canteen declared a New Yorker's night.

USS New York *leading a convoy of Battleships.*

DEPARTED	ARRIVED
San Pedro, 9-20-45	*Hawaii, 9-29-45

*Hawaii, 9-29-45; This was my last entry.

We picked up another group of high-point men to be discharged at an east coast port, going through the Panama Canal once again and arriving at New York several days later.

The Old Lady arrived in New York Harbor in time to participate in the Navy Day celebration on Oct. 27, 1945. I had the necessary points so was immediately discharged, sent by troop train to New Orleans, then back home to Gulfport, MS.

On July 8, 1948, I noticed an AP photo that showed the *New York's* destruction 40 miles SW of Pearl. She had survived two wars and two Bikini atomic bomb blasts; went down at 2:30 p.m. after eight hours of air attacks and light shelling. What a sad ending for a gallant lady.

She was a compassionate ship, known as the Orphans' Ship because she gave Christmas parties every year for orphans. Her decks had held the King and Queen of Belgium, Sultan of Morocco, movie stars, in WWI the Prince of Japan Hirohito, and the common man to whom she gave her strength and protection.

USS New York BB-34 at sea.

USS *NEW YORK* (BB-34)

Crew size: 536
Bikini Atoll Arrival: 15 Jun 1946
Bikini Atoll Departure: 22 Aug 1946
Crew Location for Shot Able: USS *Rockbridge* (APA-228)
Crew Location for Shot Baker: Rockbridge
Shot Able Location: 1,547 yards (1.4 km) ESE
Shot Baker Location: 920 yards (750 meters) ESE
Decontamination Location: Pearl Harbor
Sunk 8 Jul 1948, 40 nmi (74 km) SW of Pearl Harbor

TASK UNIT AND FUNCTION

The battleship *New York* was a member of TU 1.2.1 (Battleship and Cruiser Unit), Battleship Division 7, serving as a target vessel for Crossroads. Its crew was evacuated before each shot. Among the experimental equipment on board were food and clothing (provided by the Quartermaster Unit) and free-piston recording gauges.

Shot Able (1 Jul 0900)

30 June
1425 Crew evacuated to Rockbridge.

1 July
1430 USS *Reclaimer* (ARS-42) noted a smoldering fire amidships on New York (Reference 6, p. 7-I-A-10)
1615-1625 *Reclaimer* moved alongside New York and extinguished the fire (Reference 6, p. 7-I-A-15).
1648 Team reported the ready service ammunition on New York had overheated (Reference 6, p. 7-I-A-17).
1730 USS *Clamp* (ARS-33) sent a boarding team aboard.

1742 Boarding team returned to *Clamp*.
1750 *Clamp* reported *New York* Geiger sweet; underway from the target ship (reference 6, p. 7-I-A-18).
1847 *Clamp* reported *New York* Geiger sweet (Reference 6, p. 7-I-A-19).

2 July
1159 Commanding officer and boarding Team A returned aboard ship. No radiation detected except telephone radium marker buttons, which were not test-related.
1400 Team B returned aboard and commenced opening up the ship.
1630 Team C returned aboard.
1820 Team D returned aboard.

3 July
1130 Team E returned from *Rockbridge*.

4-23 July
Crew aboard ship.

Shot Baker (25 July 0835)

24 July
1125 Crew evacuated to *Rockbridge*.

25 July
1000-1200 Damage reported (down by stern).
1720 *Reclaimer* passed close to *New York*'s portside. *New York* was very radioactive (Reference 6, p. 7-I-B-14).

28 July
0903 *Reclaimer* again passed *New York*, which was down slightly by the stern (Reference 6, p. 7-I-B-28).
1936 CJTF I reported to Commander Rear Echelon (COMREARECH): "Further inspection of New York indicates about 1,800 tons increase in displacement with the center of gravity of additional water at Frame

40MM guns firing of Okinawa, 1945.

103, resulting in trim by stern of about four feet. Situation believed stabilized and ship in no danger." (Reference 5, p. 6-D-33).
A radiological monitor boarded and obtained a reading showing 20 minutes tolerance on deck (Reference 6, p. 7-I-B-40).

29 July
1212-1415 Washed down by ATR-40 (Reference 6, p. 7-I-B-42).
1634 A radiological monitor reboarded to take Geige readings (Reference 6, p. 7-I-B-46). Tolerance time had increased to 40 minutes.

30 July
Washed down by ATR-40 with a high pressure stream for four hours (Reference 6, p.7-I-B-48).

31 July
1550 ATR-40 reported *New York* was thoroughly foamed down using 430 cans of foam (Reference 6, p.7-I-B-62).

1 August
1025 USS *Deliver* (ARS-23) completed its inspection of *New York* (Reference 6, p.7-I-B-62).

3 August

Washed down thoroughly by USS *Preserver* (ARS-8) using high-pressure streams. *Preserver* was to report Geiger readings from about 50 feet (15 meters) before and after washing (Reference 6, p. 7-I-B-77).

5 August
1000-1500 The initial boarding team boarded the ship for decontamination operations. Maximum radiation encountered aboard *New York* was 0.625 R/hr; average reading at the time of the last survey was 0.167 R/hr.

6 August
1000-1300 Washdown prodecure completed by a tug. Captain boarded ship with initial boarding team for inspection of ship.

7 August
0800-1500 The first decontamination teams from the ship's company boarded. Four teams were used and were relieved every two hours and returned to Rockbridge. The day was spent jettisoning useless, highly radioactive materials, particularly debris and wood items. One group spent the day scouting for boiler compound, lye, cornstarch, scrubbers, gloves, boots, etc. Freshwater was provided by Rockbridge. By early afternoon water was obtained from the firemain and the topside was washed down, with particular attention being paid to the forecastle.

8 August
0800-1545 Four teams were aboard for two hours each. Necessary working materials were now assembled and decontamination on the forecastle began in earnest. Solutions of boiler compound and lye were used, and the forecastle was washed down several times. Sand was obtained and holystoning began. Cleaning up of the second deck also started and numerous pools of water removed, debris cleaned up, and hose gear straightened up.

9 August
0800-1545 Four teams were aboard for two hours each. The forecastle was again washed down and holystoned with boiler compound, lye, and sand. Freshwater still had to be hauled from Rockbridge in cans. Approximately 100 men worked on the second deck and considerable progress was made in cleaning up the second and third decks and the officers' quarters.

10 August
0800-1545 Four teams were aboard for two hours each. The forecastle was again holystoned with boiler compound, lye, and sand. Air castle and boat decks were washed down with boiler compound and lye; the main deck aft was washed down with saltwater (Reference 4).

Table A.5 shows the results obtained in reducing the forecastle's radioactivity by holystoning with boiler compound, lye, and sand.

Table A.5 Decontamination results on USS *New York* (BB-34) forecastle.

USS New York in dry dock Norfolk, VA - 1937

Table A.6. Decontamination results on USS *New York* (BB-34) topside main deck aft.

	READINGS (R/24 HRS)			
Frame #	7 Aug	8 Aug	9 Aug	10 Aug
Bow	1.6	0.7	0.7	0.6
10S	1.7	0.6	0.5	0.45
10P	1.6	0.5	0.5	0.5
20S	1.6	0.62	0.5	0.5
20P	1.3	1.2	0.5	0.5
30S	1.5	1.3	0.6	0.6
30P	1.3	1.2	0.5	0.5
40S	2.0	1.1	0.6	0.5
40P	2.0	1.0	0.7	0.5

Source: Reference 4.

The reduction in radioactivity on the topside main deck aft from one washing with saltwater is reported in Table A.6.

14-15 August
0800-1600 Four teams aboard for two hours each.

16 August
0800 Engineering party aboard to make connections to receive power from *Reclaimer*.
0830 DSM inspection parties and ship inspection parties aboard to collect data.
1115 All parties left ship except an engineering party and pumping detail.
1615 All hands clear of ship.

17 August
Two teams aboard 2-1/2 hours each.
0800-1115 Pumping detail aboard ship.
1300-2000 Pumping detail aboard ship.

19 August
Four teams aboard for two hours each.
0800-1100 Pumping detail on ship.
0830-1500 Anchor detail on ship.
1300-1600 Pumping detail on ship.

20 August
Two teams aboard for 2-1/2 hours each.
0800-1130 Pumping detail on ship.
0900-1300 Anchor detail on ship.

This is the last picture taken of the New York after being used for target practice by 2 carriers for 2 days, one sub sank her with one well placed torpedo. She capsized and sank.

Readings (R/24 Hrs.)

Frame #	7 Aug	8 Aug	9 Aug	10 Aug
70S	1.6	1.6	1.2	1.3
70P	1.2	1.2	1.3	1.5
80S	2.0	3.0	0.8	0.9
80P	1.6	3.0	1.3	0.9
90S	2.4	0.5	0.9	0.6
90P	1.7	1.0	0.9	1.0
100S	2.6	0.7	0.65	0.6
100P	1.7	0.8	0.9	1.0
110S	1.5	1.3	1.0	0.9
110P	1.2	1.5	2.0	1.3
120S	2.0	0.8	0.95	0.8
120P	1.8	1.0	0.9	0.6
130S	1.8	1.5	1.0	0.3
130P	1.6	13.0*	0.8	0.7
Stern	0.99	1.5	2.0	—

* Paint chipping. Source: Reference 4.

21 August
Four teams aboard for two hours each.
0800 USS *Widgeon* (ASR-1) alongside to starboard to assist in hoisting starboard anchor. Ordnance inspection team aboard.
0830 Anchor detail aboard.
0835 *Reclaimer* came alongside to port to furnish electrical power. Target vessel LCI(L)-615 came alongside to starboard to furnish power.
1220 *Reclaimer* and LCI(L)-615 cast off.
1235 Ordnance detail left ship.
1430 Starboard anchor was housed.
1530 *Widgeon* cast off.
1545 Anchor detail left ship. Average topside reading 0.4 R/24 hours.

22 August
Towed to Kwajalein.

24 August
Arrived at Kwajalein.

28 August
New York decommissioned.
New York was towed to Pearl Harbor, arriving on 15 March 1947. In 1948 was towed out 40 miles, shelled and bombed until it rolled over and give up the Ghost.

Shorty Reynolds hooks up a capsized Sea Plane while a whale boat crew looks on.

USS New York *(BB-34)*

Secondary battery firing off Okinawa, 1945.

Anchors aweigh - Battleship USS New York *heads for the sea. All hands are busy as the ship leaves Brooklyn, NY Navy Yard and heads for the open sea where the battle wagon will join other ships of the Atlantic fleet off Hampton Roads, VA and then return to New York in time for the opeing of the worlds fair.*

STORIES FROM THE DECK

Memorial of the
USS *NEW YORK* (BB-34)
The Old Lady Of The Fleet
by H. R. "Shorty" Reynolds

USS *New York* (BB-34) on her first mission in 1914, she was ordered to Vera Cruz, Mexico at the time of the Mexican Incident. In 1917 she was the flag ship of Rear Admiral Rodman. She joined the British Fleet and played an important part in some historical events in the German High Sea Surrender. Two of the ships crew then (1914) came aboard, I had the privilege to serve under in (1944), One went aboard in 1914 shoveling coal and was engineering comm. in 1944. The other an ensign in 1914 and was skipper in 1944, a captain.

The following are some of the statistics I took from my notes and the ships history. The *New York's* displacement in 1914 was 27,000 tons, during WWII her displacement was 34,000 tons she had a crew of 1800 or more. She steamed 123,867 miles during WWII consuming 22,367,996 gallons of fuel and expended 7,097,809 pounds of ammunition. We spent 1088 days with the Atlantic Fleet (1941-1944), we were at (Safi) North Africa Bombardment 8 Nov 1943. Earlier in 1942 she made two convoy trips to Iceland, two convoy trips to Scotland, patrol duty in pursuit of German Bismarch sunk by British. Two convoy trips to Casablanca French Morocco, in 1943-44. She had training duty in the Chesapeake and Caribbean. She schooled more Admirals, Commodores, flag officers than any other ship of the United States, over 13,000 men.

She served 276 combat days with the Pacific Fleet. Assault and bombardment at Iwo Jima, although we had lost a screw and had to limp along with one screw, we went on ahead and welcomed other newer ships in the pre-invasion bombardment. We fired 1,365,226 pounds of shells in the pre-invasion of Iwo Jima, with a colorful hit on an ammunitions storage 16 Feb 1945. We stayed the entire pre-invasion bombardment, firing more shells than any other ship present in Task Force 54.

"Old Lady"

Speaking of age, I went to Gunnery School on the USS *Wyoming*, and I am proud to say that I was aboard the *New York* when she celebrated her (31st) birthday at Okinawa where she had been for 78 days, the longest time an American war ship had ever spent in a single engagement.

She fired more than 5,600,000 pounds of shells into Okinawa, a world record. She fired more shells into Okinawa than did all our war ships in the invasion of Tarawa. She was the only one of our battleships or cruisers there not temporally put out of action by kamikaze or Japanese gunfire, yet her duties were among the most dangerous.

During one afternoon, she scored 25 direct hits on Shuri Castle. We saw the USS *Mississippi*, USS *Arkansas*, USS *Alabama*, USS *Idaho*, USS *Pennsylvania*, USS *North Carolina*, USS *Missouri*, USS *West Virginia*, USS *New Mexico*, USS *Massachusetts*, USS *Colorado*, USS *Maryland*, USS *Texas*, USS *Tennessee*, USS *Nevada*, all doing a fine job until they were damaged and had to leave

"Now hear this! Sweepers man you brooms." Clean sweepdown FO and Aft.

Standing on 14" guns while travelling through the Panama Canal. (L-R): Charles Bal, John Berrigan, and Gene Salluzzo.

for repairs. They returned, also BB-61, BB-62, BB-63, BB-64.

Japanese planes, subs, suicide boats, swimmers and planes tried to get BB-34 and once Tokyo Rose reported us sunk in Buckner Bay when we had been hit by a kamikaze on after mast and catapult in April 1945, damaging one OS2U plane and wounding two men. We lost one other spotter plane at Okinawa, the pilot was captured but returned after the war and came back aboard at Pearl Harbor.

Our pilots spotted and directed gun fire in addition to the *New York* for the 1st Marine Division, the 77th Inf. Div., USS *West Virginia, New Mexico, Mobile, St. Louis, New Orleans, Louisville, Laws, Hall, Burton, Hood, Rooks.* We received a "Job well done" from all of them. We had 206 air alerts at Okinawa. We re-armed nine times at Kerama Rhetto and Ie Shima, a tiny Island where Ernie Pyle, the famed war correspondent, was killed by a sniper.

When all of our 14 and 5-inch ammo in the area was used up, we lay in close, firing 3-inch AA at targets and at night we fired star shells so our Marines, Army and Navy could see any Japanese trying to sneak in or out. Yet with all the noise and losing sleep, life aboard the *New York* was disciplined. Capt. Kemp Christian ordered physical drill every morning from 22 Mar 1945 to 11 Jun 1945 (78 days on firing line).

The Old Lady of the fleet, the USS *New York* saw one quiet day of the bombardment and occupation of Okinawa the day President F.D. Roosevelt died, even the water was calm and the Japanese ceased fire for 12 hours.

After Okinawa we returned to Pearl Harbor where we were re-gunned completely, both 14" and 5-inch guns. The first major ship to re-gun at an advance base. Nearly ready for battle again, the war ended.

The *New York* was sent to San Pedro, CA with 850 war vets for discharge in the U.S.

We returned to Hawaii then back through the Panama Canal, bringing the old crew back to the States where we observed Navy Day 1945 in the Hudson River with President Harry Truman reviewing the Fleet.

In December 1945 we observed a tradition that started in 1915 when the officers and men of the *New York* suggest to the commanding officer that a Christmas party be given for as many orphans as the ship could accommodate. I saw a lot of little sad faces brighten in 1945 when Santa came over in a helicopter and down a rope ladder and handed out gifts. The children ate a turkey dinner with all the trimmings with us.

The story of the *New York* did not stop or end with the wars and Christmas Party, in 1945 the ship was offered to the state of New York by the Navy Dept. to be kept as a memorial, but after no decision was forthcoming after the ship had been in New York for three months, the department assigned the *New York* as one of the target ships in the Atomic bomb test.

She left New York City and the States in 1946. A handful of experienced men and officers and a green crew under the command of Capt. L.H. Bibby sailed to Bikini via California, Pearl Harbor, and Kwajalein. She was subjected to both the atomic bombs, the air burst 1 Jul 1946 and the under water explosion 25 Jul 1946.

In tribute to her builders of 1911 with a horse shoe on her keel and the Navy men who kept her in trim for 32 years, the grand Old Lady stayed afloat. The USS *Arkansas* sank, leaving the USS *New York* the oldest U.S. battleship afloat. On 28 Aug 1946, her final chapter was written when she was officially decommissioned.

Historian Remembers Ship's SERVICE AT IWO JIMA
By Denise Strub, BC Lifestyles Editor

February is acknowledged as a month of history with both Black and American history being honored.

However, during this week a world-changing series of events celebrates its 50th anniversary, the invasion and taking of Iwo Jima.

Iwo Jima is a small Japanese island in the Northwest Pacific and the largest of the volcano islands. It was annexed by Japan in 1891,

Gen. Douglas MacArthur devised a campaign of island hopping in the Pacific, which culminated in the invasion of Iwo Jima.

The island was needed as an air base to land and launch attacks against Japan. Planes could leave from the island and reach Japan without needing to refuel.

Pre-invasion bombardment began on Feb. 16, 1945, with the official amphibious assault beginning on Feb. 19, 1945.

After five days of fighting, the Marines captured the Japanese stronghold of Mt. Suribachi, which consisted of caves connected by tunnels.

American casualties, including dead, wounded and missing in action, totaled over 22,000, the Japanese lost about 21,000.

In addition to the Marines, the Navy was also a major participant in the assault,

Admiral Johnson, Lt. Col James Roosevelt, and unknown officer.

Captain Guy Davis, 1938.

with 27 Medals of Honor being awarded to Marines and sailors, more than any other single operation during WWII.

"Sometimes it seems like it (invasion) was yesterday and sometimes it seems so long ago," said H.R. "Shorty" Reynolds of Cleveland.

During the invasion, Reynolds was an anti-aircraft gunner aboard the USS *New York*. He is also the ship's naval historian.

According to Reynold's ship history, the USS *New York* joined in "pre-invasion bombardment at Iwo Jima 16 February. During the next three days fired more rounds than any other ship present, and made a spectacular direct 14"-hit on an enemy ammunition dump.

"Three days before the landing, the place looked like it was torn to pieces. They (Japanese) waited until the third wave had landed and then they came out of the rocks. They slew a lot of people," he said.

After Iwo Jima, Reynold's history says the USS *New York* went on to Okinawa in March, where "She fired pre-invasion and diversionary bombardments, covered landings, and gave days and nights of close support to troops advancing ashore."

Reynolds said during the 76 days of action, his ship was hit by a kamikaze demolishing "her spotting plane on its catapult."

Although the USS *New York* was decommissioned in August 1946 and sunk, Reynolds said her crews meet every year for a reunion.

"We even have a few who attend who were on the ship during World War I," he said.

Reynolds said he was asked to be present for the anniversary celebration in Iwo Jima but was unable to attend.

BATTLESHIP NEW YORK FACES NAVY'S WEIRD "BAT BOMBS"
STRENGTH OF TASK FORCE 38 TESTED

Pearl Harbor, July 7 (AP) The tough old veteran of the United States Fleet, the battleship *New York,* turns her armor-plated hide today to the Navy's weird new "bat bomb"— the first weapon to be used in sinking.

The 30,000 ton warship, which emerged unscathed from wars and survived two atomic blasts at Bikini, has been towed to a point 50 miles south of here to test the strength of Task Force 38.

Rear Adm. Marshall R. Greer, task force commander, said the radar-guided "bats" were used against the Japanese late in the war but, by that time, Nippon had no major ships left for targets. He said this evening's assault will be the first use of the "bats" against a ship of the *New York's* size.

"Bat" attacks also will be launched tomorrow morning. They will be followed by air, surface and underwater arms tests until the 34-year-old vessel is sunk. The *New York* is still radioactive from the Bikini tests.

GUIDED MISSILES

The Navy said the "bat" bombs are the first fully automatic guided missiles used

Kiel Canal, Kiel Germany

in combat. They are regulation 1,000 pound bombs, rigged with glider like wings and tail. They have a radar directional I mechanism which can be fixed on the target by the plane launching the bat. Radar apparatus then guides the bat into the target regardless of evasive action of the target ship.

Some 300 carrier and land-based bombers, dive bombers and torpedo planes will work the *New York* over with weapons ranging from high velocity rockets to 2,000-pound bombs. But the experts say it will take submarine torpedoes to sink the battleship.

Kiel Canal, Kiel Germany

"Awful Whipping"

"She will take an awful whipping," said Chief Storekeeper Daniel Connor of Pawtucket, RI who served on the *New York* when she was commissioned in 1914.

Connor is aboard the carrier *Boxer*, flagship of the task force, to witness the end of "Old Christmas Ship," a name acquired because of Yuletide parties given for orphans beginning in 1915 when she was in the Brooklyn Navy Yard.

Vice Adm. J.L. McCrea, deputy commander of the Pacific fleet, said the *New York's* best Christmas party was at Rosythe in the Firth of Forth in 1917. The guests then were children whose British fathers were killed in World War I.

Battle Flag of USS *New York* Given Archbishop Spellman

HONOLULU, Aug. 15.-Before the entire complement of officers and crew of the USS *New York*, massed on the forward deck under a battery of 14-inch guns, Capt. Grayson B. Carter, USN, commanding the ship, presented to Archbishop Francis J. Spellman of New York two flags, one flown aboard during the battles of Iwo Jima and Okinawa, the other used at the Thanksgiving Mass for peace, Bloch Arena. Capt. Carter spoke to his men of the courage needed to win also the peace, and expressed the wish that their flag be enshrined as a token of their bravery in war. In accepting the flags, the Archbishop promised that they would ever hang in the Cathedral of St. Patrick in New York, a memorial to the men who manned the ship during all the campaigns in which it has participated in both the World Wars.

A Happy Ship

At a signal from the captain, the band played and all sang *The Sidewalks of New York*. The song was repeated with gusto. At the sounding of six bells, came the *Star-Spangled Banner*.

The Archbishop was accompanied by Lt. J.J. Byrne of Brooklyn, present chaplain of USS *New York* and his predecessor, Lt. Daniel S. Rankin, S.M.; Capt. John F. Hugues, USN, chief chaplain, 14th Naval District, of Monterey-Fresno diocese; Rev. Eugene Morin, SS.CC, acting chancellor of Honolulu, and Rev. James Ryan Hughes, M.M., editor of the *Catholic Herald*, Honolulu.

Glorious Record

The USS *New York* is one of the most famous battleships of the U.S. Navy. Commissioned in 1914, she served as flagship under Admiral Hugh Rodman during WWI, and participated in the surrender of the German High Seas Fleet, Nov. 21, 1918. On Nov. 3, 1918, the then Crown Prince Hirohito of Japan was a guest on board. The USS *New York's* broadsides helped to bring about the Japanese surrender.

The Archbishop said: "This is a day of great joy for me-first, because I could offer Mass on the site of the sacrifice of Pearl Harbor, commemorating this day of victory and peace on the very spot where the war began.

"Now after nearly four years we have achieved victory over all our enemies. We thank Almighty God and the men and women of our armed forces and the soldiers of production on the home front.

"Likewise, I am very grateful to Capt. Carter who brought the flag of the New York to the auditorium where 6,000 of our armed forces were united in giving thanks for the victory of today.

United In Essentials

"With gratitude I receive this flag from the ship which bears the name of the state from which I come. Many of you come from this state. All of you come from that great country, the United States and that is our power.

"United in essentials, we have liberty in things not essential. I offer you as a formula for a finer world unity in essential things, liberty in non-essential things and charity in everything.

"To all of you on this ship, which has a history second to none, I promise you I shall follow Capt. Carter's words and keep this flag as a symbol of things American and of peace. I shall place it in the Cathedral of St. Patrick in New York. There let it remind us forever that the challenge of peace is just as great and important as that of war. We have another battle ahead of us—the battle for peace."

Hirohito Inspects USS *New York*

"At 4:25 H.I.H. Admiral Prince Hirohito, accompanied by the Prince of Connaught and staff came on board and inspected ship." This item of news was extracted from the ship's log dated 3 November 1918. When the USS *New York* was a ship of a girl.

In the past 27 years this ship has matured and early this spring went on a special mission to pay her respects to Emperor Hirohito. The "Old Lady" did not go on a inspection tour but instead spent 76 days throwing steel at the Emperor's prize fortress Okinawa.

When the history of the Battle of the Pacific is written the USS *New York* will have more than her name inscribed on the log, and it won't be misspelled as His Imperial Highness' name was in 1918-it appears H.I.H. Admiral Prince Yorihito.

New York Sails Into San Pedro As Dinah Sings

Amidst the strains of *"California, Here I Come,"* the USS *New York* sailed into San Pedro Harbor Sunday morning to be greeted by none other than Dinah Shore, the darling of the air waves.

Down to meet the gallant old battleship, in addition to Dinah, was the Los Angeles Police band and a bevy of beauties from the Naval Aid Auxiliary, who served donuts and fresh milk to passengers and crew.

As the New York sided into Berth 231, a beautiful with a popular tune which the crew thought was coming from a record. As the ship crept closer, a girl dressed in white, was singing from a truck. She immediately greeted the ship with, "Hello Fellows, this is Dinah Shore." A cheer burst from lined decks of the "Old Lady" and oral requests were yelled to the most popular singer of GI's everywhere.

Standing in formation to the right of Dinah was members of the Naval Aid Auxiliary, dressed in their navy blue uniforms and ready to serve the returning men with fresh milk, an item that was first on the "want" list of many.

The girls were under the direction of Mrs. T.V. Blakiston of Beverly Hills, director of canteen work for the NAA.

Following Dinah's request program, the police band entertained with several marches and ended with *The Sidewalks of New York,* one of the favorite tunes of officers and crew aboard this grand old ship.

HOLLYWOOD CANTEEN TO HONOR CREW OF *USS NEW YORK* TONIGHT

Hollywood Canteen, one of the world's most famous entertainment spots for servicemen, will honor the USS *New York* tonight with a special USS New York Night."

All enlisted men who are on liberty are urged to get a ticket before leaving the ship and meet at the rear entrance of the canteen at 1845. Buses will leave the ship at 1700.

Bette Davis will appear in person to honor the men of the New York and will have as her special guest the great pianist, Jose Iturbi, the man with the miracle fingers. Other stars have been asked to attend.

HAIRCUT BY A BUDDY
By Arnold C. Emerson

This seems rather funny now, but it did not seem so funny then. I do not remember dates, but one time when we tied up in New York, a buddy of mine and I were going ashore, but when we went to go over the gangway, they would not let us off the ship because they said we needed hair cuts.

For some reason the barbershop was closed (probably it was on a weekend or something), so we decided to cut each other's hair. We did not have good barber tools available, so we found a pair of some sort of crude scissors and went to work.

Our haircuts were not very professional, but we got off the ship and on liberty.

TRINIDAD, PANAMA CANAL, HAWAII, DATE LINE, EQUATOR, MANUS, AND THE PHILIPPINES
SUBMITTED BY NELSON G. HOKE

Morning of suicide plane: Plane came in front of *Nevada* 15 feet above water heading at our stern. 40mm hit a stop. Couldn't fire. Four 20mm's were the only guns able to fire. The *Nevada* was in the line of fire from midship guns. At approximately 200 yards, PFCs Hodgekiss, Brinkman, Bier and Chevelier, with four Navy seamen, "Ammo Loaders," started firing. At 100 yards tile plane was on fire. It banked left, then right, hitting one of our planes and going into the ocean.

I will always be proud of eight young men who saved at least 30 fellow crewmen from bodily harm, or worse. The 40mm crews came over, thanked us, and said "that took a lot of guts to stay on that plane." Thanks to all of our gun crew. Our ship was old, but our gunnery was tops. A special thank you to Capt. K.C. Christians, and

Loading projectiles, Pearl Harbor, 1945.

our officers - A very special team. I have always thanked our Lord Jesus Christ for watching over our ship and crew.

To Capt. K.C. Christian.

It makes all hands feel good to see the old veteran USS *New York* killing Japanese and smashing their weapons yourself. Your officers and crew have the highest admiration from cruiser division and making the old lady work in this war, like you never made her work in the last war.

Admiral Allen E. Smith

To Admiral Allen E. Smith.

Thanks so much for your message. She takes to it as her right, and we are only instruments to do the bidding as a host of worthy sons. We are proud of her and try to live up to her. She is the Queen and a very lucky ship.

Captain K.C. Christian

To Captain K.C. Christian

The following was received from T.F. Commander on departure from Okinawa. "Your departure would bring comfort to a lot of Japanese, were they alive to know it. Your accurate gunfire and aggressive spirit have done much to speed this campaign. Saw you do the same thing 28 years ago in the North Sea. Well Done."

MANNION'S LOG
Or How U.S. Navy Band #58
WON THE WAR!

20 Nov 1944: Came aboard USS *New York* (BB-34) (By force)

16 Dec 1944: Hit Panama Canal. Had liberty at Cristobal, Pan. (Lowest morals of any city I've seen).

18 Dec 1944: Left Panama. (Couldn't get in touch with Uncle Al.)

24 Dec 1944: Long Beach, CA. Had great New Year's and Christmas. Played terrific Dance Job.

12 Jan 1945: Left Long Beach for probable action. I am definitely not scared!

19 Jan 1945: Arrived at Pearl Harbor, met some friends from the U.S. Naval School of Music.

25 Jan 1945: Left Pearl Harbor for 24 hour General Quarters. Fired main and secondary batteries for 24 hours. I am definitely scared!

26 Jan 1945: Back at Pearl Harbor. Loaded ammunition all day.

28 Jan 1945: Left again with *Arkansas, Idaho* and three destroyers.

31 Jan 1945: Crossed International Date Line. Now a member of the "Golden Dragons."

4 Feb. 1945: Our Task Force sank a sub last night and another this morning. We lost one screw, traveling on one engine.

5 Feb 1945: Arrived at Eniwetok (Marshall Islands). Liberty horrible.

7 Feb 1945: Left Eniwetok!

11 Feb 1945: Pulled into Saipan (Marianna Islands). No Liberty!

12 Feb 1945: Left!

16 Feb 1945: Commenced bombardment of Iwo Jima.

Cardinal Spellman visits in New York harbor, 1945.

19 Feb 1945: Had burial services at sea. Band played dirge.

21 Feb 1945: Dropped blade from other screw, leaving two, two bladed screws. Making seven 1/2 knots.

22 Feb 1945: Arrived at Ulithe. Left at 1700.

23 Feb 1945: Headed toward Admiralty Island with two 1/2 blades gone.

25 Feb 1945: G.Q. Station changed to Secondary Forward, at the very top of the foremast. J.A. Phone Talker.

27 Feb 1945: Underwent all the necessary horrors and am now a full-fledged "Shellback."

28 Feb 1945: Arrived at Manus (Admiralties), entered dry-dock for repairs

4 Mar 1945: Played CPO Club on Manus. Band got drunker than skunks. Truck broke down 12:00 p.m. in middle of jungle. 300 Japanese still left in Admiralties.

7 Mar 1945: Played CPO Club again. Commander "cussed" out band for coming aboard drunk. Played terrific concert for redemption.

10 Mar 1945: Played Officers Club. All squares. Ate and drank!

12 Mar 1945: CPO Club again - Drunk again!

16 Mar 1945: Played down in dry-docks for USO Show. First time fellows have seen a white woman in five months.

19 Mar 1945: Left Admiralties in ship-shape condition.

22 Mar 1945: Arrived at Ulithe at 0630.

23 Mar 1945: Under way for another invasion.

27 Mar 1945: Commenced bombardment of Okinawa. Main Battery fired. Secondary did not. Okinawa Jima is 350 miles from Japan (Tokyo). 400 miles from Formosa (Japanese.) It had 500,000 Japanese civilians, believed to have been replaced by Japanese soldiers. It's "lousy" with artillery. It's 17 times the size of Iwo. Task Force 58 went in three days ago. Japanese broadcasts say they knew we were coming and plan to avenge Iwo. (We'll get back if we have to swim.)

Today we were narrowly missed by two torpedoes. One was launched by a torpedo bomber. The "fish" was catching up with us. We made a lucky turn. Later in the day a sub tried to hang one on us, it narrowly missed our port bow. During the night we had several air attacks. All repelled!

28 Mar 1945: Bombardment continues. Both main and secondary batteries fired. Later in the afternoon a Japanese "Zeke" snuck in painted with American insignia. He also gave the correct IFF. Luckily two of our TBF's got on his tail and shot him down. Our AA guns were firing at our own planes. The Simps!

29 Mar 1945: Today a squadron of Japanese "Vals" were coming at us. One "Val" peeled off and suicide dived at one of our escorts, narrowly missed her fan-tail. There are thousands of mines in these waters (China Sea.)

30 Mar 1945: Went to Keramo Rhetto to reload stores and ammunition. They're still mopping up. As we entered the harbor, they were still taking Japanese prisoners. They didn't look very hari-kari-ish to me. It took eight hours to take the entire island. Inside of a few hours it was converted into a fleet landing, Sea Plane Base and Fleet P.O.

Went back to Okinawa to play tag with "The sons of heaven." Received usual dawn and dusk alert.

1 Apr 1945: (Easter Sunday; April Fool's Day: D-Day) First LCIs went in - in formation.

They launched rockets around the entire island to push the Nips back away from the beach. TBFs and Corsairs from Formosa and carrier bases strafed, bombed and fired rockets. All the ships surrounding the island turned loose all they had. We threw everything but the mess cooks at them. It looked like an invasion from Mars. The island was a mass of smoke when the first wave went in. The Army and Marines established a beach head with considerably light resistance.

15 Apr 1945: Had very little time to write. Will try to summarize events from 2-15 April. We knocked down several hun-

dred Japanese planes. They sank six of our destroyers with suicide planes. They also hit two cruisers, the *West Virginia, Tennessee* and *Maryland* were all hit.

They released several hundred lepers and maniacs on the island. Our Marines tried to round them up without harming them. Most of them were armed so they had to be killed....

16 Apr 1945: Our package arrived! Last night a "Zeke" got through our AA fire and hit amidships. He ripped all the communications between the mainmast and foremast down. I was at my battle station atop the foremast when he hit just beneath us. He also destroyed our observation plane by knocking it off the catapult. Casualties were light. The crew now whistles "And the Angels Sing."

5 May 1945: Pressed for time! *Tennessee Nevada, Texas*, practically all battle wagons gone; leaving us target for tonight.

Main battery barrell replacement in Pearl Harbor, 1945.

Lately they've been using "Skunks." They're little crudely constructed boats, approximately 12 ft. long by 5 ft. wide. They're another suicide craft, loaded with two depth charges, one on each side, and a torpedo in the center. They buzz around inside our smoke screen, and when they hit all hands get off and walk.

Since my last entry many ships have been hit. Approximately five battleships (including USS *New York*, 25 destroyers sunk or damaged, four cruisers and countless merchant and landing vessels destroyed. We're shooting down planes quicker than they can build them. The ratio of planes destroyed is one to their 10.

Scuttlebutt is that we are going on another invasion about 180 miles from Tokyo or the China coast. Task Force 58 Where art thou?

25 May 1945: Our 58th day at Okinawa! No rest for the weary. There are many happenings I've failed to enter throughout the invasion, for various reasons. Such as too weak to lift a pen or too weary to see the book. More often than not we sit up all night for air alerts, or firing on the island. Last night we were on "Call Fire" from 8:00 p.m. to 8:00 a.m. Whenever the Army or Marines have their hands full, they call the Navy for assistance. We fire illuminating projectiles (star shells), over Japanese occupied Okinawa so the Army can see what they're firing at. Last night, however, we fired Point detonating fused projectiles. They're used to destroy emplacements, and the shrapnel is anti-personnel. For cement revetments and really dug in emplacements steel nose plugs do the trick. They penetrate before they explode.

Our guns (5") have lost 33.5% of their efficiency and need to be replaced badly. The Japanese are practically licked, but are still putting up stiff resistance. We're all pretty well fed up with this place and can't wait until we shove off.

All of us bandsmen firmly resolve to pop the first guy in the beezer that says a musician has the life of Riley aboard ship.

Still with all we've seen of the Army and Marines we're thankful we're in the Navy.

27 Mar 1945: Recently many Japanese raids have been picked up by our radar. As soon as they reached to within 40 miles they'd seemingly disappear into no where. Today it was learned that they were landing on a small island approximately 40 miles from here. We were kept at Air Defense all day today although the flash was white and green, (all clear). We expect a big raid tonight. The Japanese threatened to sink the entire fleet at Okinawa this week.

28 Mar 1945: Although we had 14 Japanese raids last night, none of them came to within two miles of the ship. We did have counter-battery from the beach though. A shell (3" or 5") landed within 200 yards of our port beam. Every ship out here LCIs, cruisers, destroyers, battlewagons, etc. went right in close to the beach and threw every type of projectile aboard at them. We fired 40s, 3," 5" and 14." The gun that fired at us, although it was too hazy to see, was apparently silenced. As I write this, we are at air defense. We have as many as 34 Japanese raids on our radar screen. AA fire is rampant on both sides of our ship. Perhaps this is the anticipated raid. The ship that carried our last four days mail to the States was sunk off Okinawa.

29 Mar 1945: Last night one of our Observation planes was assigned to take an Army officer 90 miles to the *Missouri*. He made the *Missouri* all right but never returned. We assume he has been shot down. We fired the 5" guns all night and expected to do the same tonight.

11 Jun 1945: Left Okinawa! After 76 days of unadulterated hell. We were at air defense close to 400 hours. For us it was a great deal worse than Iwo. Believed to be headed to the Philippines.

14 Jun 1945: Arrived at Leyte. Had no liberty. Those that did say it was "no where." Played usual concerts etc.

17 Jun 1945: Left Leyte for yard period at Pearl Harbor. I believe "Smitty" and "Chuck" Roberts are there. It will be good to see them again. Scuttlebutt says we'll pick up a new skipper soon.

29 Jun 1945: Put on Harry Brainard's show "On the Beam." First performance went along terrifically. I did a fine job of lousing up the vocal on *"You Came Along"* at the second performance. The band (Pete) rescued me and we got through it fairly well. (Practice) 30 Jun 1945, fired guns all day Put into Pearl Harbor 1600.

4 Jul 1945: Went ashore and met three Navy Bands. They wear silk shirts and have all around terrific deals compared to our happy little outfit. We'll be here about 30 days. Then - who knows?

4 Sep 1945: Since my last entry the Japanese have surrendered. The fateful day was 11 Aug 1945. We left Pearl Harbor 1 September and are now on our way to San Diego, CA with 800 passengers. They're going to the States for discharge. Our duty will be to transfer high pointers to the States and low pointers to Hawaii. Lt. Keller, the aviator who was lost at Okinawa), was found a prisoner in Japan. We have a new skipper now, Capt. Grayson B. Carter. He's a fine fellow! The band plays three times daily, marches in the morning, dance band in the afternoon, and dance band again before the movie.

When we reach the East Coast, our ship will be decommissioned. Amen! It seems silly to decommission a ship after putting new guns on her - I guess that's the Navy way!

This is the finis of my Navy Log but not the end of T.J.'s Naval career In conclusion I have only this to say - "WHEW!"

THE DIARY OF A U.S. NAVY SAILOR WWII
By George Pomeroy

June 1939: Graduated from Waltham High School, Waltham, MA, Age 18.

September 1940: Went to Boston with a classmate to look into U.S. Navy opportunities. I passed the written and physical exam. My classmate flunked the physical! (Flat feet! I can't imagine why the Navy was so interested in feet.)

October 1, 1940: Went to USN Training Station, Newport, RI. Was one in a class of 78 with CPO Bibby, a 20-year serviceman. Lots of marching drills on a large parade ground right on ocean beach. One day, CPO Bibby marched our column right into the water up to our waist (I was in the second row) before he ordered about face. Later he apologized! First and only time I heard a CPO apologize! The manual of arms with 11 lb. rifle. After 2-4 hours of this, I could not keep my arms down at my side. They kept rising upward!

In the last week of training, I was given the choice of mess duty or guard duty. Unfortunately, I chose guard duty. November was a very cold month! I walked the sea wall next to the USS *Constitution* (Old Ironsides). We also had to sleep aboard ship in hammocks, uncomfortable and dangerous The heavy oak beams were directly overhead!

December 2, 1940: Week of graduation! Came down with ptomaine food poisoning! Face, hands and feet were twice the size! Spent five days in sickbay. My classmates went to Norfolk, VA to the USS *Vincennes* and the USS *Quincey* light cruisers without me! In 1942, both were sunk in the Coral Sea battle! (There but for the Grace of God!)

January 2, 1941: Ordered to Norfolk, VA, assigned to the battleship USS *New York* BB-34, a 1917 WWI vintage ship, the largest ship I had ever seen. Seamen 2nd were placed where needed. I was in the boatswain's gang. Top side deck service. Wood decks! (Do you know what a holey stone is?) It's a brick size soap stone with a hole in the center.

A broomstick allowed you to stroke this, along with water, to wash the decks down - weekly. After a few hours, arms and shoulders were stiff and sore for days! My first General Quarters was in a 4x4 chain locker in 14" turret. This was used if the hydraulic system did not work. Two men having to move two 14" guns 180 by pulling chains! They promoted me to the powder room, which wasn't much better! 4x3 powder bags, six men, no air!

March 1941: Shakedown cruise to Guantanamo Bay, Cuba and the islands of Puerto Rico. (Lots of fun riding Burros over islands and visiting Blue Beard's Castle. Carved my initials in the bar.)

Do you know what a Section 8 is? That's an unfit for duty discharge from the service. How do you get one? By wetting the bunk every night! By jumping overboard every evening at movie call. One sailor jumped every night from the starboard side,

Turret 4 firing at Iwo

Heavy Seas!

swam around the stern of the ship and came up port side gangway. I don't know if he got his discharge, but I do know that he never was "man overboard" while the ship was under way!

Movie call was interesting to a novice like myself. The trailer shown prior to the movie was always a warning about socializing with prostitutes and the medical ramifications of this dangerous sport! (this was enough to scare the dickens out of a kid just out of high school!)

May 5, 1941: Convoy duty - New York to Newfoundland, Nova Scotia, Iceland. Battleships, (2) Cruisers, (2) Destroyers, (6) Freighters, Tankers, Supply Ships, 25 in all. Cold, windy, fog, rough seas. four crossings in all, 1941 to 1942. Iceland (2) and Scotland (2). Lots of submarine wolf packs in the N. Atlantic. Could not stop for survivors. Fire and oil all over the seas. (There but for the grace of God!)

Iceland has 20 hours of sunlight. One tree in city of Reykjavik surrounded by a steel fence. Very barren land! We landed Marines to replace English soldiers. The English did not like this, as they had made girlfriends and had wives in the two years they were there.

Scotland, a beautiful land and people. We anchored in the Firth of Fourth at Grennock near the Port of Glasgow. You have to take a train to Glasgow. Six passenger compartments, two sailors and two very pretty girls ended up in a dance hall, and had a great time. The girls were sisters, so we took them home and met their parents, who gave us a very late supper of scrambled eggs.

The next trip to Scotland we took a duffel bag of two dozen eggs, bacon, oranges, apples and coffee to their parents. All of these things were in short supply for these nice people in Scotland.

Changing of officers in the Pacific. From Captain to Carter.

USS *NEW YORK*

Had several nights as a lookout on the fan tail of the ship. Observing a towing spar about 100' aft in the waters just ahead of the following ship. In cold and foggy weather, with night glasses it was difficult to see the spar. These were used to separate ships in line with each other. There was no radio communication allowed, only visual contact.

I volunteered with three other shipmates to crack eggs for the cook's galley. 1500 men X 2 eggs each equals 3,000 eggs (I wonder how long it took an average housewife?). This was each Friday night for Saturday's breakfast. The big reward was all the fresh, hot bread, rolls and butter, cakes and pies. The *New York* had the best bakery in the Atlantic fleet.

August 1, 1941: Transferred to VO-5 aviation group - 15 men and 3 pilots, 3 OS2U mid-wing observation planes. Catapulted off and picked up when flown. (I lied a lot to get this transfer!) The flights were six hours, very cold and difficult to use a relief tube when wearing heavy flight suits. One morning, we took off in Newfoundland at 9:00 a.m. in sunshine and returned at 3:00 p.m. in solid fog. Had to use the circular honing ring tuned to the USS *New York*. Had to land in bay where a cruiser, several destroyers and the hospital ship S.S. *Mercy* was also anchored. (This was a real tight fit, but we made it.)

October 1941: Two weeks at Quonset Point, RI. A brief week at Quonset Point NAS in Rhode Island allowed us to fly daily under the Narragansett Bridge, "lots of fun" until the Coast Guard complained and we had to stop.

November 1941: Portland, ME: Anchored in Casco Bay wintertime, six hours of liberty. Had to take a long boat to get ashore, two miles. Cold and wet. Spent the time ashore at a local USO. Lots of nurses from the hospital to talk to. (Never left the USO, two feet of snow and very cold!)

December 7, 1941: Pearl Harbor Day, I had just arrived home on leave after a trip to Iceland on convoy duty. Dad woke me up Sunday morning and told me to come down stairs to listen to the radio (no TV in those days). President Roosevelt gave his Day in Infamy speech and Congress declared WAR on Japan! Several days later a telegram arrived and instructed me to return to NAS, Norfork, VA. Went to Boston with Dad to South Station Railway. Police were all over the city of Boston. We were waved through every intersection on the way. I guess all service men were recalled and the police assisted them. Trains were loaded with service men returning to duty. Arrived at NAS and was issued a 45 automatic and placed on guard duty at the aircraft hanger. (After I shot a hole in the hanger roof I learned how not to handle a 45 Colt automatic!)

After 30 days we were once again aboard the *New York* and headed out to North Atlantic. Two trips to Scotland during 1942 was very cold and very rough seas.

The signs of the convoys were increasing now and more equipment was going to England. The German submarines were on the prowl and tension very high among the personnel. Ice was four inches on decks, superstructures and aircraft. We had to use axes to reduce ice in many instances. One aircraft on stern of the ship had a broken wing and we could not fly most of the trip because of the weather.

January 1942: Spending several days in Scotland was a big relief for everyone. As I mentioned previously the people were just wonderful to the U.S. sailors.

October 1942: Entire VO5 from USS *New York* (157 men) transferred to Norfolk, VA again and to the USS *Sangamon* CVE-26, a ESSO oil tanker conversion to escort carrier. Carried F4Fs SBD and TBDs. Picked up my air crewman wings at NAS, Norfolk, VA.

Characters That I Met: A shipmate who slept with eyes wide open! Another who never took a shower or washed underwear or mattress cover. We had to escort him to the shower, clothes and all, and wash him down using scrub brushes! Another whose snoring and talking in his sleep kept the compartment awake! We used clothes pins and tape! A sailor that virtually said nothing. "Silent

Divers go deep to untangle a cable

Sam" we called him! Another who was a real Bible thumper from Georgia. Two brothers named McCoy from the Tennessee hills, members of the feuding Hatfields and McCoy clans. A shipmate that we called "Foo Foo" who had a locker full of after shave lotion and antiperspirant.

Personal Habits, Every sailor had a large bar of green castille soap, washed everything with it! Worked especially good in a salt water shower. Grease spots were eliminated by carbon tetrachloride. Dungarees, not Levis, with bell bottoms were towed to a line and towed overboard while the ship was on its way, this got rid of the new look and they always fit better! The white hats were always pulled down on the sides, looked real "salty." The Air Force did the same thing with their caps, of course they wore ear phones over the caps, that was their reason for looking that way. Navy issue shoes were all black, polished up beautifully but had to have rubber soles added to prevent slipping over board. Uniform blues and pea coats were all wool and did not fit too well. When I made first class petty officer I bought a pair of tailor made gabardine blues. $40, my whole months pay! But, boy did I look and feel good!

Having been married 56 years to a wonderful girl, mother and grandmother, having two wonderful children, three grandchildren and two great-grandchildren, we have been blessed, and as I have said previously, (there but for the Grace of God!) Thank you, Lord!

November 28, 1942: A Marine schoolmate and our girlfriends went to Boston for ballroom dancing. The Coconut Grove Ballroom was our destination, however, the line outside was so long and a police officer advised us there was no chance of getting in to the ballroom that night. So instead we went to the Roseland Twin Ballrooms. When we came outside at the end of the evening we heard the sirens and saw the red skies in the direction of the Coconut Grove. That fire killed over 600 people.

If I may, for one more moment, I would be amiss if I did not mention the brave men of the Merchant Marine that convoyed to Europe, North Africa, the South Pacific, the materials of war, food and personnel to fight this war. These men braved the oceans without defense, facing the elements of the seas and weather, knowing that survival was virtually impossible if torpedoed. The ever presence of Hitler's U-boat fleet. The wolf packs of the Atlantic, Japanese subs of the Pacific. Must have been enormous. These men who died or lived never received a veteran's benefit. Or a Veteran's Day. We owe them so much, and we thank them today along with all wartime workers!

MY TIME ON THE NEW YORK
BY NELSON B. PRICE

In April 1944, my identical twin brother, Henry Price, and I received our notices to report to the Navy, but we were permitted to complete our final months of high school. By the time we were called back on August 2, 1944, we were reassigned. There were several hundred boys going through the line for assignment. Henry was assigned to the Navy and I was assigned to the Army. When I found out that my brother had been assigned to the Navy, I went back in, blocked the whole line, and told the man at the desk that my twin brother was in the Navy and he was going to put me in the Navy as well. He said he wasn't going to change it and even if he did we wouldn't be together. I looked around and saw an empty chair against the wall. Since I hadn't been sworn in, I told him that I was not refusing to go in the service, but I was going to sit in that chair and I was not going to move until he put me in the Navy. He said he hated to do it, but he would go ahead and assign me to the Navy-which he did.

Henry and I boarded the USS *New York* the same day and served together for the remainder of the war. We were one of five sets of twins aboard the *New York*. During our time on the ship we even obtained the same ratings on the same day. Henry was assigned to the #4 turret and I was assigned to the #5 turret. Many times we were mistaken for each other.

Ships orchestra in "Salvo Concerto" on the firing line. Okinawa, spring, 1945

Once, the 4th Division officer saw me in the 5th Division and chastised me for being there. It took some time to convince him that I had an identical twin on board. Many times Henry and I covered for each other when one of us was a little bit late getting back from leave. It was easy since our shifts were different.

Our first day on board some boxing gloves were brought out by Boson Mate Saul and he motioned to me to put on a pair. He chose another man to don the other set and said, "We are going to have a little recreation." I knew nothing about boxing at all, but I had done a lot of scrapping with my brother. So I lit into the other guy with all I had. He took off in a beeline to the boson mate who stopped the fight. The boxing gloves were never brought out again.

On our way from Norfolk to Panama we hit some rough water. A big wave came over the side of the ship and took the man next to me right off. It knocked me down, but since I was behind the gun shield, I was not swept off. We could not stop for him, so one of the ships behind us maneuvered and picked him up without stopping. He was returned back to the ship when we arrived in Panama.

I vividly remember Christmas, 1945; the *New York* hosted a party for an orphanage in New York, The Brooklyn Home for Blind, Crippled and Defective Children. Many of us were assigned a special child to show around the top side of the ship and to make sure they enjoyed themselves. Many of us enjoyed this as much, if not more, than the children. That is an occasion I will always remember and cherish.

One night while I was on watch everyone was tired and sleepy. We had been firing the guns most all day and loading ammunition at night. One Marine sentry who was assigned to walk around the edge of the deck went to sleep and walked off the side of the ship. He was brought back onto the ship, but he had to pay for his rifle.

At Iwo Jima, the *New York* scored a direct hit on a Japanese bunker, which was behind heavy steel doors. The shell got there just as the doors opened and blew the bunker up. *The New York* fired more shells at Iwo than any other battleship. We fired so many shells that we eventually wore the big guns out and had to return to Pearl Harbor and get refitted with new guns. We were set to return to battle and "fall hunting season," but the war ended before that happened.

We went through numerous air raids at Okinawa. Many times the Japanese kept us awake all night. One night on watch, we heard an airplane and reported it. Word came back that it had to be a friendly plane as there were no enemy planes in the area. About that time two bombs went off about 500 yards from the ship. The ship shook like a leaf and sailors came pouring out to man the guns; some had nothing on but their shorts. While at Okinawa, the *New York* was hit by a Japanese kamikaze that destroyed the ship's spotter plane, but otherwise did little damage.

The most somber moment of my time on the *New York* was when wounded personnel were brought on board. Three of these men died and were buried at sea.

MEMORIES OF "THE QUEEN"
Written by Lt. Joseph S. Thompson, and Submitted by Marie A. Thompson

My father Lt. Joseph S. Thompson (deceased August 2000) served as a gunnery officer on the New York from 1943-1945. In 1997 he had printed a selection of true stories from our family's history. In that collection he put down some of his memories from the USS New York and they are as follows:

The Seas Shall Give Up Their Dead

After the first day of the landings on the black sand beaches of Iwo Jima, because of the tremendous numbers of wounded, many of the casualties had difficulty being ferried out to the hospital ships USS *Hope* and USS *Consolation*.

At evening of February 17, the day after the landings began, one of the landing craft handling the wounded came alongside USS *New York* and requested that we take aboard seven Marine casualties for medical attention in our sick bay. They were brought aboard and given immediate attention by Navy surgeons. All were critically injured but struggled to survive. One died early the following day, and two more followed during the midwatch.

By close of the next day the Marines ashore had driven clear across the four and one-half mile width of the island and ship bombardment was no longer required. The commander of Task Force 38 then ordered USS *New York* to depart Iwo and obtain repair to one of our propellers that had lost a blade during the days of heavy firing.

The next morning, some miles southeast of the battle zone we prepared for burial at sea of the three deceased Marines.

The ship's forecastle was cleared and the bodies, each wrapped in canvas with a 5-inch shell inside the wrap to insure the body's sinking, were brought on deck. A slide had been prepared at the ship's side to deliver the bodies into the sea after the burial rites.

A Navy burial at sea is a solemn occasion and usually is conducted by the ship's captain. Our ship was fortunate to have a chaplain assigned so Lt. Cmdr. Dan Rankin, the chaplain, conducted the ceremony in the presence of the captain and executive officer and others of ship's company. A six-man detail stood by to move the bodies after Father Rankin read the words of the Navy service: We now commend you to the sea where you shall find peace until the last day when the seas shall give up their dead and at the judgment you shall have eternal rest.

One after the other the Marines slipped into the blue-gray water. A great calm had come upon the East China Sea. It became all of a sudden, a tranquil, spot where short days before so much commotion had taken place in the sulphur fumes and steaming waters of the Kazan Retto, the Volcano Islands. The peace of burial at sea seemed a fitting reward for those who had fought at Iwo.

The command "all engines ahead full" was given and Iwo Jima soon was lost astern on the horizon.

Crossing The Equator

Crossing the equator at sea meant rising from the level of a pollywog, one who had never experienced the event, to the level of shellback, a friend of King Neptune, lord of the sea, and his sidekick Davy Jones, who maintained an enormous locker in the deep, in which refuge could be found by ships and men lost at sea. USS *New York*, en route Iwo Jima to Manus, Admiralty Islands, crossed the equator at 145 degrees East Longitude on Feb. 27, 1945 at approximately 3 o'clock in the morning, in the Navy midwatch. Preparation for initiation ceremonies for 1,700 personnel of 2,300 in the ship's company began on the previous day. An excerpt from a diary describes the happenings:

Feb. 26: The master-at-arms voice came over the loudspeaker, "At eight bells in the morning watch all hands will lay forward

Some shots of the cross the equator celebrations and some shots for Harold C. Champeau's listing.

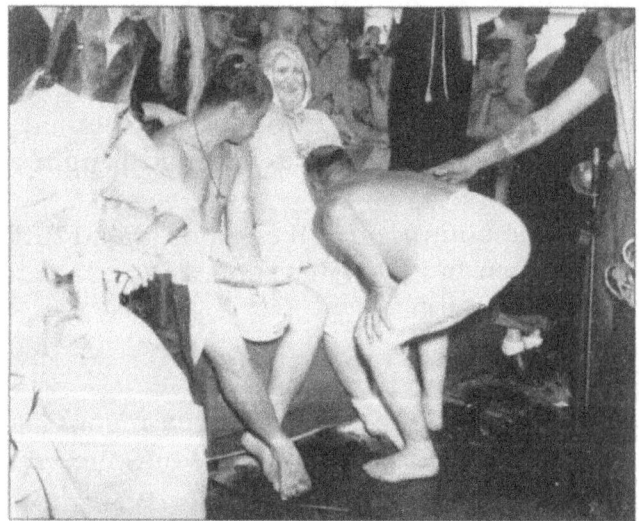
BB Albert Jr. a.k.a. Queen Aphrodite - Iwo Jima to Manus.

More shellbacks - Ring leader in this picture is unknown.

Shellback initiations - going to Manus for screw replacement.

Shellback ceremony - crossing the equator enrout to Manus.

to welcome aboard Davy Jones and Peg Leg the representatives of Neptunus Rex." With these words the first day of a two-day celebration of our crossing the equator began. Jones and Peg Leg and a "pirate" crew were greeted on the forecastle by Captain Christian. We will not cross the equator until about 0300 tomorrow the 27th.

Feb. 27: The Jolly Roger the black flag with skull and bones of piracy was hoisted. The only time I ever saw it at sea. At eight bells in the morning watch King Neptune, his queen and the Royal Baby, the Royal Chaplain, the Royal Doctor, the Royal Barber, and Royal Police (all of whom were shellbacks from earlier cruises) "came aboard" and held court. Initiation of all hands began, commissioned officers first. A most visit recollection of the initiation was walking the plank, blindfolded, with hands fastened behind, and stepping from an actual plank, and falling some 10 feet into a large tank of water. This afforded an opportunity for members of an officer's division to allow him to thrash about in the tank for a considerable time or to be dragged out sooner. The diary recorded that Lieutenant Shellenberger suffered a fractured arm and head injury as he walked the plank and was later sent to a base hospital at Manus. Initiation of the crew soon started.

The Royal Barber was directed to several whom it was believed would be improved by a full haircut. Others required facial improvement furnished by stripes of black paint. Some were considered infants and stretched on the teak deck for diapers to be attached by the Royal Doctor, the Royal Police prevented anyone from leaving. All were furnished certificates vouching for their initiation and signed by Davy Jones and King Neptune.

At daybreak Feb. 28, 1945 Manus appeared, a heavily jungled island some 60 miles in length with high mountains along its spine, and a curving shore protected by barrier reefs from the tides of the Bismarck Sea.

MANUS

At sunrise February 28, USS *New York* steamed into Seeadler Bay, a great harbor lying between a curving arm of Los Negros island and Manus, a much larger island at the end of the curving arm. Both were included in the Admiralty Island group, in the Bismarck Sea in the Southwest Pacific. A one-gun salute indicating we had been observed, came from HMS Black Prince, flagship of the Royal navy squadron of Sir Bruce Fraser that New York had orders to join. We acknowledged the shot with a round from our 3-inch-50 battery and proceeded with our escort destroyers USS *Conklin* and *Corbesier* to the fleet anchorage and dropped anchor. Three U.S. destroyers, USS *Cassin, Young,* and *Leutze* had arrived prior to our coming. There were seven ships of the Royal Navy there: besides *Black Prince,* two battleships, HMS *George V* and *Howe,* a cruiser, HMS *Invincible*, two destroyers HMS *Avenger*, and *Argonaut* and a supply ship HMS *Reaper*.

Regular ship routine on *New York* continued until 0730 when the captain's gig was hoisted out, lowered and manned by a coxswain and bosuns mate third. A ladder was rigged at the rail. At 0800 Captain Christian and Chief Lieberman his secretary, a chief yeoman, descended the ladder to the gig and proceeded to *Black Prince* to pay the captain's respects to Admiral Fraser and determine any orders he might have. At about 0900 both visitors left the British ship and proceeded to the dock area to visit the U.S. commander and decide when *New York* could enter dry dock to have two propeller blades replaced, our reason for visiting Manus.

When Captain Christian returned he had information that the ship could enter dry dock the following day. Liberty for the starboard watch was declared at 1300 and those in that watch prepared to explore the port. A diary gives some idea of the place:

February 28: Manus lying about 120 miles off the north coast of New Guinea in the Bismarck Sea is a land of narrow coastal

Crew scraping the ship on Manus Island.

plains on which most of the Navy structures are built. Behind a range of foothills, and ranging blue in the distance rise heavy shoulders of mountains. A tracery of eucalyptus groves outline ridges some 3,000 feet above the sea. The equatorial sun, three degrees south, lies heavy all about, and the air is thick with heat. A dozen airy sailboats lie in a basin formed by a reef, and green-blue water foaming at the edge of a line of palms makes a lovely picture. A few sails move about the lagoon and soon a large white diamond of canvas moves before the wind out from the shore. It is of the type developed by the Papuan natives of this region for use in their war canoes. It is called a prau with outrigger to balance the craft and a diamond-shaped triangular sail slung between two slanted spars. Some have bright scarlet or green sags. The one that came close aboard our launch had a crew of about ten blacks. An old fellow in the cockpit, wearing a headdress looked at us and waved a hand. Then others crowded the rail waving. Americans seem to have made a good impression on the natives here who are known as Negritoes.

March 1: The equatorial regions emphasize that the tropics are a land of clouds. Ever present south of the Tropic of Cancer clouds outdo each other along the equator. Tonight (in the first night watch starting at 2000) a classic thunderhead forms in the south, with evidence of a great thermal updraft along its sides. Soon it towers jet-black seemingly above all creation to the open areas far above, the land beyond the moon. In the morning watch rosy pink and gold fluff shows in the horizon at sunrise every day without fail. The whole country down here gives an air of immense breadth and width and tremendous spreads of stars at night. As though a mighty hand had drawn aside a curtain revealing a vastness of sea and air totally unknown before. Sean O'Casey, the Irish playwright, tells us in his drama of politics and rebellion, *The Rising of the Moon*, that "all action begins at the rising of the moon." The moon's actual rising in the land of the Southern Cross is a scene worth viewing whenever the chance occurs. The diary goes on:

March 2: Moonrise comes about 2000, and begins with a few blood-red slashes of light behind a low-lying cloud, inky on the horizon. Rays change quickly to a pale lemon hue that floods upward into a lighter mist where the moon itself soon appears. It races overhead and long before the watch ends disappears into cloud again. A few months later, during the Okinawa campaign, the rising of the moon, then called "bombers moon" was a sight to be decried, as the bright rays revealed our fleet in Nagagusuku Wan, the bay where suicide planes from southern Japanese airfields brought fire and death to many.

STILL AT MANUS

March 5: The islanders here, some of whom work in and around the base, come arrayed in red and green and blue sarongs, men only. Usually the top of their woolly head is bleached with a concoction reputed to kill head lice and that leaves a portion of the hair in a reddish blonde condition. Their average height is rarely more than four feet almost pygmies, although the many inches of wool atop their heads make them appear taller. Not all come to work. Some walk single file looking neither to right nor left, wrapped each in his bright blanket carrying a long thin-bladed knife or sword, and at times a spear. The metal blades and spear points, not locally available are alleged to have come, over decades of time, from Arab traders who came across the Indian Ocean to trade for whatever was desirable.

These indigenous people, somewhat different from the New Guinean natives, are said to be cannibals, eaters of "long pig" (usually their enemies). The coast tribesmen whom we see appear to have forsaken this practice. In their outrigger sailing craft, if not on the beach, they seem to be more than a little friendly, waving and grinning under their strange triangular sails.

March 6: Received three lovely letters from Grace and one from Mom. Grace had heard via radio news of our being "in" at Iwo Jima, and sent clippings from the *Star*. Perhaps my post-battle letter mailed at Ulithi will reach her soon.

March 9: Knox was killed today. He died in sick bay about 2015 with general paralysis from a broken neck. He was crushed by the ramp of a landing craft while on the beach for a softball game.

March 18: The rains at Manus are getting to be endless and the rainy season is setting in. Went to a receiving ship, USS *Crescent City,* to review a draft of men recently arrived to obtain a chief yeoman for the Executive Officer, Commander Hansen. Navy personnel brought out from the States are distributed from receiving ships at forward bases. I was told that *Crescent City* before the war was the President Lines cruise ship *Del Orleans* loaned to the Navy by the shipping line. This was a common practice after start of hostilities and recalled to me a similar situation involving HMS *Benbow* occupied by a British admiral as his headquarters at Port-Of-Spain when *New York* was based there. *Benbow* had been the American yacht *Dixie* owned by a New Orleans family that had it tied up at the Sugar Wharf in New Orleans at Mardi Gras in 1941 when my bride photographed it while on our honeymoon. Later it was loaned to the U.S. Navy and transferred to the British in a lend-lease deal. Aboard *Crescent City* a chief yeoman was chosen and we both returned to our ship.

March 19: Repair completed for New York, released from drydock, all boilers lighted off and got underway for Ulithi at 1800 in company with USS *Cassin, Young, Leutze* and HMS *Reaper*.

ALL IN A NIGHT'S WORK

It was late afternoon in October 1945 and the USS *New York* was seven days out of Pearl Harbor bound for Balboa, Panama Canal Zone. A third of the crew had been transferred to allow 1,050 passengers to board, Army, Navy and Marines ready for discharge when we reached port. The weather had been reasonably good though a hurricane was reported off Costa Rica

The finished job - officers standing below the ship are unknown.

which we could avoid by staying to the south. Lieutenant Commander Connell, the navigator, was anticipating San Jose light in the Gulf of Panama within a day's time if all went well. He had completed his noon position fix several hours earlier and estimated the ship to be 440 miles northwest of Cape Blanco, Nicaragua, and somewhat east of Clipperton Island, a rookery of tern and frigate birds in the south central before the storm. A heavy groundswell appeared shortly after sunset brought by the hurricane to the east, and at 1830 a radioman handed the captain's marine guard a message. It was from Navy Command at Balboa ordering a change of course to the northeast to intercept a cargo ship and to take aboard one of its crew who had gone berserk and was causing extensive difficulty. The new course would take us very close to the hurricane path and extremely heavy seas, which would make the task of taking aboard a passenger a dangerous obligation.

Our initial test would be to locate the cargo vessel in the darkness. The order had furnished a position where the vessel had been several hours previously, but even though it was dead in the water, the wind and heavy swells would cause it to drift. Our 1940's radar was designed primarily to detect incoming aircraft and was of little help in this case.

By 2130 we were coming up on the given position and our two searchlights flared up into the night sky to give our position to any lookout within visibility. Two red rockets soared up to starboard some three miles off and soon *New York* had the craft under searchlights. She was *Jean-Baptiste LeMoyne,* a United States freighter out of New Orleans for Yokosuka, Japan with supplies for the new destroyer base there.

A very heavy sea was running by that time, and to avoid a possible collision *New York* lay off some 300 yards from the other ship. That distance was too far for a breeches buoy to be rigged, by which the patient could have been sent a shorter distance to our ship on a double cable. A motor whaleboat was lowered by *New York* with a lieutenant, bosuns mate, and coxswain with two deck division seamen to manage the 26 foot craft. Captain Carter hoped to avoid boarding, so it was agreed that the patient would be strapped to a gurney or stretcher if available, lowered over the side of LeMoyne, and hopefully taken aboard the whaleboat.

At that point the sea was lifting and dropping the whaleboat 10 to 12 feet as each swell was mounted on the 300 yard journey. The coxswain at the helm kept the craft headed into the swells to avoid swamping, and at length came alongside the freighter as another problem became apparent. The swells that tossed the whaleboat also caused LeMoyne to pitch, but at a different interval as the ship was so much larger and displaced much more water than the whaleboat.

While one craft rose on a swell the other was falling and the freighter sank much deeper than the small boat. Thus at one moment the whaleboat would be within perhaps eight to 10 feet of the ship's rail

USS New York - George Pomeroy in the face mask and goggles.

but a few seconds later it had dropped 10 feet, with the ships rail far above as the ship was rising. The coxswain with his years of experience finally brought the two close enough for a seaman to catch the end of the gurney with a boathook and dragged it into the boat as the sea pulled the craft away. A crane on *New York* easily lifted the whaleboat aboard after the return trip and the patient taken to sick bay. He was not violent at the time of exchange and was sedated by the medical staff.

After the excitement most of the ship's company retired to their bunks but Lieutenant Thompson had the midwatch from 12 until 0400, so after relieving the watch he had time to mull over the seaman's adage that in the service one does not have to look for work - he is surrounded by it. And a ship always is on call - for a night's work.

BIG GUN EXPERIENCES
By Randolph Terrell

At Iwo Jima we were given a number of wounded men that had their ship blown out from under them. One was a man of 17 or 18 from Boston. He had a small wound in his stomach that had given him no chance of recovery, and the doctors had given him pain killers. As he lay in a bunk about a dozen us stood around him trying to cheer him up when he raised his hand wanting to speak, "I appreciate your trying to cheer me up, but I know I am dying for a good cause, and I know you will carry on." He died the next day on my 18th birthday and was buried at sea.

While at Okinawa we used up our 14" shells but our captain moved us in close to the beach as if we were in search of a target. Workers on the West Coast were on strike so we had very little in our magazines when President Roosevelt died. We checked and found that we had six bags of powder and one shell total. We sought to fire our last shell with a 5" shell as a memorial to him. There was a miss fire and we had to fire again. Our guns were worn out since we had fired 1-1/2 times the limit on our guns. We had started taking off the point

Way down in the docks.

detonator fuses and replaced them with dummy nose plugs and you could see the shells going end over end into the beach where they would explode by their base fuses. I thought how some Japanese must have seen a shell that they thought was a dud when it blew up.

Our 5" guns were so worn out that the men would put a shell in the guns with a bag of powder and run to the other side of the ship before firing the guns because they didn't know which end of the gun the shells would be coming out. There was no hydraulic rebound left. The springs would allow the guns to slowly be bound.

After the end of the war we took a number of men from California to Hawaii. On one trip a gunner's mate was servicing five of our 20mm guns when a pair of new officers stopped and one of them reported that he had never seen one fired. The gunner's mate informed them that the gun was not ready to fire. The young officer knew what he was doing and strapped himself in and began to fire. After a few rounds the gun's barrel, which was not locked in, went over the side. The young officer asked why he

"The Flying Fisherman" Ensign Smith and Lt. Comd'r Virgil Lagaly. On the bridge enrout Pearl Harbor to New York. Oct 1945.

was not informed that the gun's barrel was not locked in. The gunner's mate told him, "You said you knew what you were doing and I didn't argue."

As I think back at my experiences aboard the *New York*, my thoughts often go back to how tired our men got at Okinawa.

I remember waking aft one night and saw the man in front of me walking slower and slower until he went to sleep and fell on the steel deck—and didn't even wake up.

On another occasion, I was eating when our rations were down to potato soup for breakfast and dehydrated potatoes filling the large section of our troops for lunch and supper. A sailor sat down in front of me and I thought he was asking a blessing when he fell forward into his tray and his face went into his potatoes. The man next to him grabbed him by his hair and pulled him up. He reminded me of someone who had been hit in the face with a pie.

I tried to do my best but one time I almost ended up in the brig. My bunk was on the third floor and I stood watch by a bunch of valves that would flood the magazines in case we were hit. One night on the 12-4 watch, I just couldn't keep awake. I reported to my watch in my underwear and went to sleep on a table. I was able to answer to the chief on my phone every hour and a chief came by on the half-hour. When he came by at 12:30 I was asleep on a table there. He cursed me out but when he left I resumed my sleep. The same thing happened at 1:30 and 2:30. When he came back at 3:30, he dragged me off the table and pulled me down to C&C where the officer of the watch was. We found him sound asleep so he couldn't turn me in.

We were not allowed to sleep during the day time but we found ways of getting around that. One way: in the passage way by our sleeping quarters there was a fowl weather locker where heavy outfits were stored for cold weather. We would get inside with out nose up against the louvered front and get someone to lock us in and we would sleep standing up.

SAGA OF THE FLYING FISH
By Robert F. Smith

One beautiful October morning in 1946, as the USS *New York* headed west and home, Lt. Virgil "Legs" Lagaly, officer of the deck, and Ensign Bob "Friendly" Smith, his junior OOD, saw an incredible happening: schools of fish with wings flying over the ship's dipping and rising bow.

Said Legs, "Friendly, go to the foc'sle and catch one for breakfast."

Friendly, still amazed at the sight, did just that, bare-handed.

One of our shipmates (46 years later) sent the negatives to Friendly's roommate 2nd Lt. Paul Merideth, USMC, who had prints made in time for our 1992 Reunion at the Kingsley Inn near Birmingham-Bloomfield, MI.

More recently, the saga took life again as Christine Kess, owner of Seattle's unique Flying Fish Restaurant, on hearing this "can you believe it" fish story, requested the picture. Hopefully, by the time you get to her place, you will find it as part of the decor, properly captioned for that improbable West Pacific dawn.

A 30 DAY TRIP
By Eugene Salluzzo

When I was on the USS *New York* going through the Panama Canal, we picked up a special force of U.S. Army jungle fighters to bring them to the Philippine Islands. This was about a 30 day trip and I ran into a soldier that lived close to my home town, Hoosick Falls, NY. He lived 20 miles north of me in a small town named Greenwich, NY.

His name was Harry Brophy and he was sleeping in the bottom hammock of the five tier hammocks. He was seasick for 30 days and never got out of the hammock. I made it a point to feed him candy bars for the whole 30 days until we got to the Philippines. When I was discharged from the Navy I found where he lived and visited him frequently.

About a year ago, and after I hadn't seen him for a while, I was in this famous restaurant in Greenwich, NY named Wallies. I asked the proprietor if Harry Brophy would be around and she said "No he died but his brother is right over there." I went to the brother and told him what I have just written here and he remarked, "You killed him, he died a sugar diabetic."

A SHOE REPAIRMAN
By Dominick Rocco

I was in my junior year of high school when I joined the Navy. I had a trade when I joined and it was shoe repair. My dad died when I was 7 years old and my dad's brother was a shoemaker and taught me the trade. When I went aboard the USS *New York*, I had a shoe repair shop aboard the ship and repaired shoes for 1,600 men onboard.

The USS *New York* was stationed in Chesapeake Bay. We took midshipmen to Trinidad and back, then went through the Panama Canal into the Pacific Ocean. We went to the Marshal Island, then to the invasion of Iwo Jima. The Marines of the 3rd and 4th Division went in. It was hell watching them take a beating. We won a citation for blowing up a huge ammunition dump. It went off for hours. I hurt my shoulder when I was blown 10 feet into an electrical box.

We went from Iwo Jima to Okinawa and spent 89 days of shelling the hell out of that island. We took a kamikaze on our flight pad and knocked out one of four planes.

We started for Japan when the atomic bomb was dropped, ending the war. Thank God.

USS New York and Normandie anchored at Fort de France, Island of Martinique.

Two-thirds of the 7A AA Gunners Division - H. R. "Shorty" Reynolds is the first man staning on the left.

Front row center: Lt Peyton, Cprl Husdale, Lt Powers

USS *NEW YORK* (BB-34) SHIPMATES

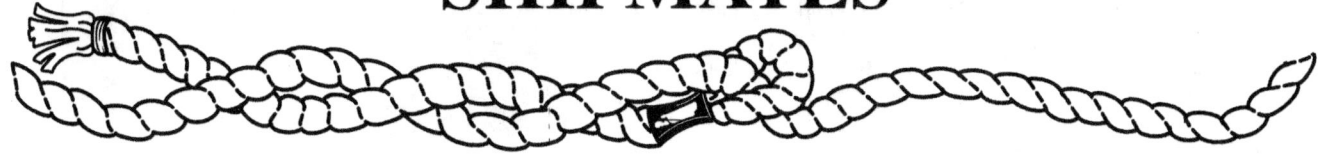

BENJAMIN B. ALBERT JR., GM3/c, born Sept. 13, 1924 in Roanoke, VA. Graduated Thatcher High School, Thatcher, AZ in 1941 and Roanoke College in 1949. Attended Washington and Lee School of Law, 1949-50 and recalled to USAR in August 1950. Received a MBA from Syracuse University in 1963 and remained in the US Army until 1979 when he retired as colonel 0-6.

Served aboard the USS *Milwaukee* as S1/c, 1943-44, until ship transferred to Russian navy in Munmansk, Russia March 1944. Served aboard SS *Warfield* May-August 1944, Normandy invasion, GM3/c; upon return to CONUS USS *New York,* September 1944 to April 1945.

In September 1944, 10 men were transferred to the USS *New York* from remaining crew of the USS *Milwaukee*, but he remembers only two besides himself, Lester L. Johnson, then GM3/c and now CPO USN retired, and Robert Carpenter, then GM3/c, now deceased.

On the USS *New York*, there were only 60 shellbacks who had crossed the Equator on other ships. After Iwo Jima operation, the *New York* broke four blades of the starboard screw and had to proceed to Manus Islands in the Admiralty Islands to go into dry dock and await arrival of two new propellers.

En route, they crossed the Equator and those 60 shellbacks had the job of making 1200 pollywogs (never crossed Equator before) into shellbacks.

While at Kerama-retto Island, Okinawa in April 1945, he was injured by two 14-inch projectiles coming together and removing two-thirds of the tip of his right thumb. He was rewarded by being sent back to San Diego to attend Advance Gunnery School and ultimately being discharged as a GM3/c in April 1946.

HAROLD I. ANDERSON, born in May 1926 in Reading, PA. Enlisted April 26, 1944 and attended boot camp at Camp Peary, VA. Boarded the USS *New York* at the Norfolk Navy Yard in September 1944. Assigned to S Division, attained rank SK/3c and was a storekeeper in charge of the canteen, clothing and small stores.

His battle station was 20mm AA on the mainmast. Participated in the invasion of Iwo Jima and Okinawa. He will always remember his first trip through the Panama Canal, the Equator initiation and the Christmas party for the orphans in New York City.

Disembarked May 1946 in San Francisco and received an honorable discharge June 2, 1946 at Bainbridge, MD.

Worked 33 years as a sales representative for Nestle Food Co. and retired in January 1985. He spent 24 years in politics as a township commissioner and school board member. He was president of fine arts board for 14 years and still lives in Reading, PA. His wife and he like gardening, traveling and visiting their grandchildren.

HENRY H. ANDERSON, born Nov. 7, 1922 in Morristown, NJ. Enlisted in Hoboken, NJ and served in the Okinawa Campaign in the US Navy Reserve as engineering officer. He obtained the rank of ensign.

Retired from Union Carbide Corporation as a design engineer in the Plastics Division, Bound Brook, NJ. He serves as a volunteer in charitable and service organizations and enjoys woodworking, music, gardening and family correspondence.

He married Phyllis Quimby on June 14, 1947. They have seven daughters, two sons, four grandsons and seven granddaughters.

CHARLES E. AULT, QM3/c, born Nov. 3, 1913 in Akron, OH. He moved to a farm in Doylestown, OH April 1, 1922 and attended school there. At the age of 17 he enlisted in the US Navy at Cleveland, OH with his father's signature.

Sent to Great Lakes in February 1930, assigned to the USS *New York*, San Pedro, CA in June 1930. Served as gun striker, No. 1 turret in 1931 and quartermaster striker in 1932. Commanding officer was Capt. Husband E. Kimmel and commanding navigation officer, Walter S. Delaney. In the 1930s the Navy went to the tropics for war games. Discharged in October 1934 at the Brooklyn Navy Yard as QM3/c.

Attended Ohio State University 1938-40, farmed 1940-50 then worked for Westinghouse Electric Corp. until retiring in 1972. He still works as a marketing manager for telecommunications.

Married Mary Lou Deibel in August 1947 and they have three children: Charles, Joseph and Christine; 11 grandchildren and one great-granddaughter. They attended the USS New York reunion that was held in St. Louis.

KLINEDALE J. BAKER, born May 8, 1923 in Culver, IN. Enlisted in the Navy Nov. 4, 1942 in Chicago, attended boot camp and Hospital Corps School at Great Lakes, IL, graduating Feb. 5, 1943. Transferred to Naval Hospital and then to South Annex, Norfolk, VA. Ordered to the USS *New York* Feb. 19, 1944 and served aboard until January 1946.

He went to the Pacific in November 1944, through the Panama Canal to Pearl Harbor then headed for Iwo Jima. Left Iwo Jima with two broken propellers. After repairs, the ship proceeded to Okinawa. They were at sea for 76 days, then returned to Pearl Harbor after the war to bring back troops.

Memorable experiences include passing through the Panama Canal, viewing Mt. Suribachi, the hit they received from the kamakaze, burying three men at sea, the Christmas party for Orphans on board the ship in 1945 and the review of ships by President Truman in New York, Navy Day, Oct. 27, 1945. His most outstanding memory was being initiated as they crossed the Equator and becoming a shellback Feb. 27, 1945. The chief surgeon aboard was initiated and his finger was dislocated. As a corpsman Baker tried to reset the broken bone but was unable to do it. They called the chief medical officer to repair the damage and healing began to take place.

Returned to New York in 1945. Discharged at Great Lakes, IL Jan. 20, 1946 as PhM1/c. Attended Indiana University graduating in 1949 with a degree in public health.

Employed at Indiana State Board of Health for 21 years and retired from the USFDA in Washington, DC after 23 years in 1993. Married Jane Kemp, a WAVE in WWII, on June 14, 1950. They had four children: Teresa Jane Pratt, Gregory James (deceased), Phillip Michael and Marianne Ball; grandchildren are James, Christopher, Sean and Jonathon Pratt; Jason, Hannah, David and John Baker; Jeremy, Sara and Zachary Ball. Baker and his wife retired to Deltona, FL in 1993, he enjoys gardening, fishing and genealogy.

JOHN E. BESSETTE, MoMM1/c, born Dec. 4, 1919 in Pawtucket, RI. Enlisted Jan. 15, 1943 at Providence, RI. Assignments included NTS, Richmond, VA (diesel); NTS Grove City, PA (Advanced Diesel School); USS *New York* and Iwo Jima, Okinawa.

Awarded WWII Victory Medal, Good Conduct Medal, American Theater Medal and APCM w/2 stars. Discharged Feb. 10, 1946 at Boston, MA, MoMM1/c.

He recalls a sailor being washed overboard, Feb. 9, 1944, and rescued by a destroyer.

Bessette's mother received a Navy Citation from the Secretary of the Navy, James Forrestal, Oct. 19, 1945 for having five sons in the Navy: Philip, Alfred Jr., John, William and Gilbert.

Retired Dec. 4, 1981 as a mechanical supervisor assistant general foreman from Boston & Maine Railroad. He spent 41 years working for the New Haven Railroad, Penn Central Railroad and Boston Main Railroad. He is President of National Assoc. of Retired and Veteran Railroad Employees, Unit 32, Providence, RI.

Married Mary Cunningham Feb. 19, 1949 and they have five sons: John, Michael, Thomas, Timothy, Richard and seven grandchildren: Scott, Ashley, Amanda, Lily, Jennifer, Kimberly and Michael.

JACK H. BELL, S1/c, served aboard the USS *New York* (BB-34), 1944 and 1945 at Iwo Jima and Okinawa. He served aboard AM-159, 1945-46 and was discharged at Mayport, FL.

ROBERT J. "BOB" BIGELOW, Fire Controlman S1/c, born Aug. 19, 1926 in Paris, MS. Enlisted in May 1944 in Memphis, TN and was inducted in June 1944. Attended boot camp at Camp Peary, VA, where dogs and sailors (in that order) were not allowed on lawns in Williamsburg, VA.

He went aboard the USS *New York,* fire controlman S1/c, at Norfolk, VA about 1600 and worked all night loading stores getting ready to sail on the tide. His time with the New York is the same as Henry R. "Shorty" Reynolds except that Shorty forgot to mention their riding out the typhoon off Okinawa and getting a hole big enough for a couple of elephants to walk through in their starboard bow. He nearly drew submarine pay on that one. Bob's twin brother, Ralph A. (deceased) served on the BB-34 with him until he was discharged in early 1944 as yeoman 3/c.

Bob was discharged in June 1946 from regular Navy at Millington Air Station, TN, but stayed in the inactive reserve for a few years. Awarded APCM w/2 stars, WWII Victory Medal and Combat Action Medal.

He is a life member of the DAV, AFSA, NRA, TREA, American Legion, John Wayne Cancer Foundation and the American Battleship Assoc. He is also a 32nd Degree Mason, a Scottish Rite Mason, Shriner and commander of the Pacific Northwest Shrine Assoc. Legions of Honor (2000-2003).

Married Margaret Ann July 15, 1949 and they have four children: Cathy, Wayne, Randy and Cris, and five grandchildren.

EVERETT BURNETT, born March 5, 1923 in Cordova, AL. Enlisted Dec. 30, 1941 and attended training in Norfolk, VA. He attained coxswain rating while aboard the USS *New York* and fought in North Africa, Iwo Jima and Okinawa. Served as ammunition loader; main job aboard was manning a 14-inch gun turret.

He served with Dale Chandler in 5th Division and went home on leave with him in 1943 where he met Dale's first cousin, Aline Marie Pharris. They were married Nov. 10, 1945 and have two sons, Wayne and O'Neal; three daughters: Donna Mickle, Linda Williams and Darlene Isbell; 13 grandchildren and 10 great-grandchildren.

They reside in Warrior, AL and part-time in Gulf Shores, AL. His main hobby is fishing and also likes telling stores of his days in the Navy. He is a very proud WWII veteran.

THOMAS J. CASA, enlisted in December 1941 in the US Navy, Syracuse, NY. Attended boot training in Newport, RI and US Navy Radio School at Noroton Heights, CT. Reported for duty in April 1942 as a radio striker on the USS *New York*. While aboard the *New York* he participated in the invasion of North Africa (Safi) and aboard the *USS Prevail* during the invasion of Salerno and Anzio.

Following that duty he was assigned to the Fleet Administration Office, Portsmouth Navy Yard with the rate radioman 1/c. He was discharged in November 1945 at USNTC, Sampson, NY.

Enlisted in the US Naval Reserve in 1948 and was recalled to active duty during the Korean War and assigned to USS *Kyne*. Discharged in June 1952 at Brooklyn Navy Yard.

He was employed by General Electric Co. as a product service radar technical representative for many years, then employed

in the US Merchant Marine, shipping out as a radio electronics officer, working on board oil tankers and freighters. Retired in November 1984.

Married to Elizabeth for over 54 years and they have two children, Michele and Michael; five grandchildren: Michael, Elizabeth and Katharine Allan and Jake and Alexandra Casa.

LEWIS B. CAWTHORNE JR., Seaman 1/c, born July 20, 1926 in Raleigh, NC. Attended Raleigh Public Schools and graduated from Hugh Morson High School. Enlisted in the US Navy June 10, 1944 and had basic training at Camp Peary, VA. Served only on USS *New York* and left ship in San Francisco just before it left for Bikini Atomic Bomb Test. Discharged May 26, 1946 in Charleston, SC, Seaman 1/c.

After getting out of the Navy, he attended college a couple of years, worked as railway mail clerk 3-1/2 years, then went to work on the railroad. He retired from Csx as locomotive engineer after 40 years.

He married twice (both wives are deceased) and lives at Surfside Beach, SC. He travels around the country as much as possible.

HAROLD C. CHAMPEAU, born March 5, 1919 in E. Braintree, MA. Enlisted in the US Navy in 1937 and served as a signalman aboard USS *Nitro*, USS *Maryland*, USS *Edison* (on convoy duty in the north Atlantic, replacing the torpedoed USS *Ruben James*), PC-492 (on convoy duty to Brazil when promoted to chief signalman) and USS *New York* (on battle duty in the Pacific, including the battles of Iwo Jima and Okinawa). He was discharged in 1945.

Received BA, Magna Cum Laude from Clark University and MA from Northwestern University where he was a graduate teaching assistant. He had a doctoral fellowship in Russian studies at University of Maryland. Transferred to the University of Michigan where he was a PhD candidate and studied Chinese at Cornell University the State Department Language School in Taiwan.

He was in the US Foreign Service and served in Panama and as an American consul to Hong Kong and Macao. Later he was the agricultural attaché to Warsaw, Poland and Hong Kong.

After retiring from government service, he was an assistant director for the National Council of US-China Trade. Later he was a consultant on China and an importer of Chinese beer.

Presently retired he is living in a Maryland suburb of Washington, DC with wife Beverly.

DALE CHANDLER, Chief Turret Captain, born Aug. 22, 1922 in Jeff County, AL, where he attended elementary school and graduated high school at Mortormer Jordan. Enlisted in the US Navy Oct. 27, 1941 and attended recruit training at Norfolk, VA.

Went aboard the *New York* Dec. 12, 1941 and did convoy duty in the north Atlantic. He was in the North Africa invasion in November 1942. Served as an instructor training men in main battery for 18 months. In 1944 he went to the West Coast and took part in bombardment of Iwo Jima and Okinawa. Returned to Pearl Harbor where the ship was re-gunned for preparation for invasion of Japan. Discharged Dec. 30, 1946, Chief Turret Captain.

After 30 years he retired from Drennen Motor Co., Cadillac Division. Married to Ila Mae Brasher and they have one son and three grandchildren. He has attended several New York reunions.

EDWARD P. COUNTRYMAN, born March 7, 1926. Enlisted June 8, 1944 at Alabama City, AL. Assignments included phone talker and lookout at Iwo Jima and Okinawa.

Discharged Feb. 18, 1946 as seaman. Served in USNR June 16, 1948 to June 15, 1953. Awarded American Area Camp Medal, APCM w/2 stars and WWII Victory Medal.

Retired from Lockheed Georgia Co. as plaster pattern maker. He is a Scottish Rite Shriner, 32nd Mason and enjoys traveling and gardening.

Married Shirley June 27, 1952 and they have two children, Pamela and Suzette, and three grandchildren: Brian Lawson, Jennifer and Andrew Mitchell.

ARNOLD C. EMERSON, Fireman, born Oct. 3, 1922 in Albion, PA. Graduated from West Springfield High School, PA in 1940. Enlisted in the US Navy Jan. 13, 1941 in Buffalo, NY. Attended recruit training in Newport, RI and Engineering School in Dearborn, MI and Great Lakes, IL.

Assigned to USS *New York* at Portland, ME in September 1941, serving as fireman. Transferred to USS *Tillman* (DD-641) May 28, 1942 and took part in North African campaign at Casablanca. Boarded the USS *Sigourney* (DD-643) at Bath, ME June 29, 1943. After commissioning and shakedown cruise, they headed for the South Pacific. He took part in 13 Pacific campaigns, including Battle of Leyte Gulf. Spent 1946 at Green Cove Springs, FL, decommissioning ships. Discharged Dec. 31, 1946 at Jacksonville, FL as chief water tender.

He worked for 30 years in the postal service, retiring in 1979. Now he stays busy in various social activities in his area of Pennsylvania.

JOHN L. EMHOFF, GM3/c, born July 28, 1923 in Stafford Springs. Enlisted July 5, 1943 in New Haven, CT. Cruised between South America and Africa aboard the USS *Milwaukee,* September 1943 to February 1944. The ship was sent to Russia where it was given to them by President Roosevelt in secret.

He returned to England and boarded the USS *Leyden*, a riverboat, to pick up men from the invasion of Normandy. He returned to the US on the *QE2* and assigned to the battleship USS *New York* at Norfolk. Sailed through the Panama Canal for the Pacific Theater.

Memorable experience was when they were anchored off Okinawa and he was surprised to meet his brother who was in the Seabees. His brother had spotted the ship and took a Navy duck out to meet him on the *New York.*

After the battle of Iwo Jima an Okinawa the war ended and he returned to the US on the *New York.* Discharged in February 1946 as GM3/c. His ship is now on the bottom of the Pacific Ocean after being used as a bomb test.

Retired in February 1985 as a printer from New Image Printing, Manchester, CT. He is a member of the American Legion and Master of Stafford Grange No. 1.

Married Maude Meyer March 2, 1946 and has four children: John Jr., Timothy, Eric and Karen; eight grandchildren:

John III, Jeanne, John II, Charles, Sarah, Allison, Hannah and Jessee.

ROY E. GAINES, born April 14, 1926 in Hartwell, GA. Enlisted June 9, 1944 and attended boot camp at Camp Peary, VA, then assigned to USS *New York* (BB-34). Participated in Iwo Jima and Okinawa campaigns.

Memorable experience was taking a kamikaze plane on his birthday, April 14, 1945, at Okinawa; also memorable are the two lifelong friends he made during his service years. Discharged May 27, 1946 as fire controlman 3/c (Main Battery). Awarded American Area Campaign Medal, APCM w/2 stars, WWII Victory Medal and Good Conduct Medal.

Owned and operated a radio and television station in Toccoa, GA, retiring Jan. 1, 1995.

Married Evelyn Fowler on Aug. 31, 1947, and they have two children, Connie and Stuart, and one grandchild, Crayton. His hobbies are golfing, fishing and woodworking.

RUDOLPH HENRY GENTGES, USS *New York* (BB-34), Fireman First Class, born January 15, 1913 in Frankenstein, MO. Attended St. George Elementary School in Linn, MO. He enlisted in the United States Navy in 1935. He graduated US Naval Station, Great Lakes, IL, November 20, 1935.

Served entire tour aboard the USS *New York*, December 1935-November 3, 1939. Company 9, First Battalion. He served with the following shipmates: Brown, Baker, Burgess, Childester, Flock (from NE), Harper, Hunter, Jones, Kline, Moses, Sanders, and Stein (from AZ).

He received Seaman First Class on September 21, 1936 with marks of 3.89 rating. His commanding officer was Commander Ware.

He attended the coronation of King George VI, and Queen Elizabeth in 1938.

He attended the New York World's Fair, U.S. Fleet Days, and marched in the parade on May 1 and 2, 1939.

He received honorable discharge as Fireman First Class, under Commander O.L. Downnes, on November 3, 1939. Discharge number C232334.

After his tour on the *New York* he went to work for Wagner Electric as a duty engineer in the power plant in St. Louis, MO.

On December 14, 1941, he enlisted in the merchant marines aboard the US *Cantonfield* in the Engineers Corp and hauled supplies and oil during WWII in both the Atlantic and Pacific theaters.

At the end of the war, he started his own business with his brother, Hugo, US & Gentges Roofing and Insulation in 1948 in Jefferson City, MO. He retired from Gentges Roofing and Sheet Metal in 1978 after 30 years in business.

He married Vida C. Morris Rushing on October 19, 1940. They have two children, John D. Gentges, Sr. and Nancy Rushing Backes. They have nine grandchildren: John Gentges Jr., Julie Gentges Clingman, Jerry Gentges, Janice Gentges Houser, Jodie Gentges Maddox, Karla Backes Pettigrew, Greg Backes, Tim Backes, and Lisa Backes Michel. They have 23 great-grandchildren. They currently live in Jefferson City, MO. Rudy and his wife enjoy camping, fishing, and relaxing with their family.

JAMES T. GOFF, FC2/c, enlisted in the Navy after graduation from high school in Seminole, OK and went through boot camp at San Diego, CA. He went to Range Finder School at San Diego and was then sent to the receiving station at Norfolk, VA. Went aboard the *New York* (November 1942-June 1945) and made the North African invasion.

Left the ship while at Okinawa and went to Advanced Fire Control School at Washington, DC. Upon completion of the school he was sent to the Naval Academy at Annapolis for 18 months instructing midshipmen in fire control. Transferred to the destroyer USS *Wilson* (DD-847) which operated between Newport, RI; Key West, FL and Gitmo, Cuba.

After leaving the Navy in 1948 as FC2/c, he worked at selling oil field supplies for over 35 years and now lives in Las Cruces, NM with his wife Ina. They have a son, daughter, three grandchildren and five great-grandchildren.

FLOYD A. HAGE, GM2/c, Gun Captain 40mm, born Oct. 5, 1916 in rural Hamilton County, IA. Attended school in Hamilton County and after finishing school worked as a farm hand. In 1941 he attended sheet metal school in Des Moines, IA. Upon completion of training moved to San Diego, CA and worked at Consolidated Aircraft Co.

Enlisted in the US Navy June 1942 and received recruit training at Great Lakes, IL. After five weeks of training he was sent to Pier Six in New York City and three weeks later transferred to Norfolk, VA and assigned to the USS *New York*, GM2/c, gun captain, 40mm.

His most memorable moments include: November 1942, the invasion of Africa, bombardment of Safi; Nov. 11-12, 1942, Fedala Harbor where six ships were torpedoed but no damage to the *New York*; March 21, 1943, convoy duty to Casablanca and manning the rails for an official visit from the Sultan of Morocco; Nov. 21, 1944, ship sent to West Coast passing through the Panama Canal; Feb. 16-18, 1945, bombardment of Iwo Jima; Feb. 27, 1945 crossed the Equator and became a shellback; March 27, 1945, 76 days in the Okinawa Campaign; July 1945, R&R in Hawaii and Sept. 2, 1945, Japanese surrender (he had shore patrol duty that night).

He served aboard the USS *New York* until his discharge at Wold Chamberlain Airport at Minneapolis, MN Oct. 1, 1945. Upon discharge he worked for Dodge dealership for 30 years as a mechanic, then for the city of Ames for 10 years. Retired Oct. 1, 1978.

He and his wife have lived in Ames, IA since October 1945.

GEORGE NELSON HAMER, S2/c, born March 8, 1925 in Columbus, GA. Graduated from Central High School, Phenix City, AL in 1944. Entered the Navy in June 1944 and attended boot camp at Camp Peary, VA.

Boarded the USS *New York* in September 1944 at Portsmouth, VA and assigned to the 4th Division. Served aboard her through Iwo Jima and Okinawa. Discharged February 1946 at Charleston, SC, S2/c. He played football on Norfolk Fleet team in 1944.

Graduated from Troy State University, AL in 1950 with BS degree. Taught and coached for 36 years, 29 of those at Bartow Senior and Junior High School, Bartow, FL. Retired from Polk County Schools, Bartow, FL in 1983, but coached football through 1988.

Married to Joyce Middlebrooks in October 1950 and they have two children, Georjan and Gregory, and four grandchildren: Katie, Andrew, Jacob and Rebecca Cauthan.

MATTHEW C. "HANK" HANCULAK, GM1/c, born Oct. 23, 1922 in Cleveland, OH. Enlisted Oct. 23, 1940 at Cleveland with boot camp at Great Lakes.

Assignments include USS *New York*, six convoys – North Atlantic Patrol (New York, Iceland, Nova Scotia and Scotland); (1942) North African invasion; Safi Harbor, Canary Islands (Occupation Casa Blanca); (1943) USS *Sangay*, South Pacific area; Funafuti; (1944) Te Bua Bua Channel; Marshall Islands; Eniwetok and Efate; Seadler Harbor, New Guinea; Palau Islands, Kossol Passage, Caroline Islands; Task Force 38; (1945) Ulithi, Kwajalein; USS *New York* (TDY), pre-invasion, Iwo Jima; Okinawa invasion and occupation; (1946) USS *Juneau*, South Atlantic, Caribbean Operation.

Discharged Dec. 10, 1946 in Boston, GM1/c, Master at Arms. Awards include Bronze Star, Navy Commendation, Combat Action Ribbon, PUC, two Good Conduct Medals, American Defense Medal, American Area, EAME, APCM, Navy Occupation, WWII Victory Medal, total 10 Battle Stars.

Memorable experiences: hearing FDR speak to them before the North African invasion; the violence of the North Atlantic Ocean and the beauty of the South Pacific.

A union carpenter, 40-year member of the VFW, R.I.P. June 10, 1980. Married Helen and had three children: Thomas, James and Carol, and seven grandchildren: Nick, Matt, Tom, Jamie, Mike, Steve and Emily.

MARVIN G. HENAGIN, Coxswain, born Nov. 13, 1920 in Buffalo, MN. Attended elementary schools in Los Angeles, CA and high school in Holland, MI. Enlisted in US Navy in 1939 and attended recruit training at Newport, RI.

Served aboard the following ships: USS *New York*, Jan. 5, 1940-June 18, 1942; attained coxswain rating while on the USS *New York*. Served on the USS *Arkansas* (BB-33) June 18, 1942-Oct. 13, 1943. Following a 30 day leave, he went aboard the USS *Pinto* as BM/1c, Dec. 29, 1943. Left USS *Pinto* for transfer to Lido Beach shipyard for commissioning of ATR-6.

Transferred from ATR-6 to ATR-56, Aug. 21, 1944. Left Norfolk, VA for Philippines Sept. 21, 1944. Promoted to chief bos'n mate, acting appointment while serving aboard the ATR-56 in the Pacific.

Sailed from Philippines Oct. 29, 1945 for San Francisco, CA. Received honorable discharge at USNTS, Great Lakes, IL.

Worked as auto mechanic 22 years and retired as production supervisor from Parke-Davis Co. after 17 years.

He and his wife now enjoy boating on Lake Michigan and attending two battleship reunions a year.

JOHN HLADIK JR., EM1/c, born Nov. 17, 1922 in Perth Amboy, NJ Graduated Woodbridge High School and enlisted in New York City in July 1942. Attended boot camp in Newport, RI. Attended Morehead State College, electrician's mate program and attained EM3/c rate.

Served on USS *New York* (BB-34) from January 1943 to February 1946. Discharged from Lido Beach Separation Center in March 1946.

Graduated Rutgers University and also attended Newark College of Engineering. Married in November 1946 and has two sons. He was employed at Union Carbide as plant electrician and instrument engineer for 45 years. Retired in 1986 and resides in Edison, NJ and Zephyrhills, FL.

NELSON G. HOKE, Cpl., born April 2, 1924 in North Ilion, NY. Enlisted Dec. 14, 1942 at Syracuse, NY. Assignments included: Parris Island; Portsmouth, VA; Sea School; USS *New York* (April 15, 1943-Aug. 3, 1945); Iwo Jima, Feb. 16-18, 1945 and Okinawa March 27-June 11, 1945. He recalls captain orderly, 20mm gun instructor with Cpl. Werstak.

Discharged Nov. 7, 1945 at Parris Island with the rank of corporal. Awarded the AFEM, APCM, CAR, GCM, SSDR, New York State Medal of Merit w/Silver Shield and WWII Victory Medal.

Employed as cam maker making blades for jet engines and retired Feb. 13, 1986 from Utica Drop Forge. Married Mary on Sept. 23, 1950. He enjoys traveling, hunting and fishing.

HOWARD D. JACKSON, EM1/c, born Jan. 10, 1922 in Roodhouse, IL. Enlisted April 26, 1941 at St. Louis, MO. Received recruit training at Great Lakes, IL and attended Electric School at St. Louis Sept. 1, 1941. Assigned to USS *New York* Dec. 12, 1941 and served on two convoys to Iceland, two convoys to Scotland, North African Invasion, two convoys to Casablanca, Iwo Jima, Okinawa.

Assigned to the USS *Tidewater* Oct. 1, 1945 in Charleston, SC and to Green Cove Springs, FL maintaining moth balled LSTs Nov. 1, 1946. Discharged April 26, 1947 at Jacksonville, FL.

He worked in the electrical trade after his discharge as a journeyman electrician and electrical supervisor in major Illinois Power Co. power plants. Worked as operations and maintenance supervisor on Kwajalein in the Marshall Islands 1972-73. Retired Jan. 10, 1985 as electrical supervisor from Central Illinois Public Service Co. He enjoys riding his bicycle, fishing, boating and landscaping.

Married Olga on Aug. 9, 1945 and has four children: Wayne, David, twins Connie and Carol; eight grandchildren and three great-grandchildren.

N.W. JORDAN, one of eight children and lived on a farm in Layafette County, MS; finished eighth grade at Riverside then moved to Oxford and graduated from Abbeville High School. Entered into active duty June 7, 1944.

Served on USNT ADG, USS *New York*, USS *Missouri* and USS *Wyoming*. He was in the Pacific and participated in the invasion of Iwo Jima and not one man was lost during the battle, but one man was killed on shore. While waiting on shore after liberty, the ship's gate was let down and fell on the sailor. He was buried at sea.

Discharged Jan. 12, 1946 at New Orleans, LA and awarded APCM w/2 stars.

Attended Bricklaying School in Memphis, TN and worked several years as a bricklayer. At that time brick was not used very much, so he quit and started working at E.L. Bruce Co. He worked 30 years and retired as maintenance supervisor at Grayson Sawmill in Grayson, AL. He is an active member of the VFW and American Legion and served as commander for several years.

Married Inez McMurtrey and have two daughters, Shelby June and Carolyn Wayne.

LESTER L. JOHNSON, GMG3, 6th Division, born Jan. 5, 1924 in Mississippi. Attended school there until joining the Navy Jan. 8, 1941. After boot camp at Norfolk, VA, he was assigned to USS *Milwaukee* until she was turned over to Russia in 1944. Went aboard USS *New York* in September 1944.

With a 10-day leave, he married Lorrayne Bingham Oct. 24, 1944. Left Norfolk aboard the USS *New York*, went to the Pacific and served through Iwo Jima and Okinawa. Left the ship in Pearl Harbor and went to Gunnery School in San Diego, then to Bikini for the bomb test. Honorably discharged at Treasure Island Nov. 19, 1946. Discharged from active reserve July 1, 1976 as GMGC.

Retired from construction work and resides in Memphis, TN. Enjoys gardening, reading, fishing and golf.

Lorrayne and he have three children: Betty, Patty and Lester; three grandchildren: Victor, Kerin, and Lorrayne.

JOHN W. KAMPE, arrived aboard the *New York* (BB-34) from the BB-33 and stayed aboard the *New York* until the Bikini bomb test and final deposition.

He did inspections after tests; helped reset anchor on last tow to Kwajalein, A Division, refrigeration, ice machines; stood watches in smoke watch engine room, fire room, generators, forward torpedo room, air compressors, heating and machine shop evaporators.

Earned rating to chief machinist mate, anchor engineer on entering and leaving port. Engineered 40 foot launches and captain's gig.

He will be attending the September 2001 USS *New York* (BB-34) reunion in Washington, DC.

EARL HOWARD MANN, RM1/c, born Sept. 16, 1921 in Syracuse, NY. Attended Jordan High School and joined the USNR V3 in 1939. In the summer of 1940, he transferred to USNR Com Unit, Syracuse to NTS, NOB Norfolk. Completed basic training and stood radio watch at NAM Radio Norfolk.

Transferred to the USS *New York* and participated in US Fleet maneuvers off Puerto Rico. Served aboard the USS *New York*, North Atlantic convoy escort to Iceland and United Kingdom in 1940-42. Promoted to RM2/c, then RM1/c. Copied high-speed Morse code transmissions for ship's daily newspaper. In charge of Radio Central and radio watch personnel.

In 1943 he transferred on special TDY to Flag complement, heavy cruiser USS *Augusta* for Allied landings at Morocco. The *Augusta* had nine-hour running sea battle with Vichy French cruiser off Casablanca. He returned to the USS *New York* at the end of Moroccan campaign. Transferred to sub chaser SC1021 (nucleus crew) at Stamford, CT. SC1021 to Panama via Key West (shakedown). Then based CocoSolo, CZ, tracking U-boat activity in western Caribbean for a year. Operated via ports in Guatemala, Honduras and Colombia.

In 1944 he transferred to Brown shipbuilding, Houston, TX (nucleus crew, USS *Stafford* DE-411). *Stafford* went via Panama Canal, San Diego, Pearl Harbor to Philippines joining the 7th Fleet. Took Kamikaze (shot down others) at waterline. Structural damage could only be repaired at Mare Island, NY. It took three months to the crew's delight. Returned to Okinawa and did ASW patrols until war's end.

Received an honorable discharge at Sampson NTC went via "Frisco October 1945.

Employed 1946-47 as radio officer, US Lines Liberty ship, powdered coal cargo, trips to France. In 1947 he worked at Press Wireless, Hicksville, LI, NY with same big transmitters that sent the news he copied aboard BB-34. Next he was employed by CIA Communications, Washington, DC area bases, communications supervisor. In 1955 he worked in transmitter design engineering at GE Syracuse, later in mobile radio design at Lynchburg, VA (six years) included in 30-year GE career.

TOM MANNION, S1/c (Mus), born April 2, 1926 in Corona, NY. Enlisted Jan. 15, 1944. Attended the US Naval School of Music, Washington, DC and served in USS *New York* (BB-34) and USS *Tarawa* (CV-40). Participated in action at Iwo Jima and Okinawa.

Discharged May 21, 1946 and awarded American Theater Medal, APCM w/2 stars and WWII Victory Medal.

He owned and operated several auto repair shops. Retired Dec. 31, 1988 but still owns "Flagship" shop as retirement income. Enjoys woodworking, music and traveling.

He married Pearl on Oct. 31, 1945 and they have three children: Tom Jr., Catherine and Daniel; five grandchildren: Dawn, Deanna, Shane, Anna, Patrick and one great-grandchild Bryan.

JOHN A. MERCER, born March 7, 1924 in Litchfield, IL and attended school there. Enlisted November 1942 in Washington, DC. His first school was US Navy School of Music in Anacostia as a drummer. First assignment was the USS *New York* serving in the Atlantic. One hour before sailing to the Pa-

cific, he was transferred back to the School of Music. His next assignment was to Treasure Island, CA.

When peace was declared he had enough points and mustered out in California in April 1946. He was regular Navy as musician third class. President Carter was in one of the Annapolis trips on the USS *New York*. The *New York* friendships have lasted all these years.

After the Navy he attended school and became a cabinet maker and worked the trade for 52 years.

Married Geneva Hermsmeyer in April 1945. She was Navy also, only just as a civilian. Four sons completed the family, one Army, one Air Force: John Jr., Thomas and twins David and Richard; seven grandchildren: Charlie (Navy), Brian, Jason, Heidi, Geoffrey, Andrea and Trevor (Air Force)

He retired to Reno, NV and spent his most enjoyable time in his workshop. He lost his battle with diabetes March 9, 2001.

DENNIS F. MURPHY, S1/c, born in Brooklyn, NY. Enlisted in the Navy in December 1943 and attended boot camp at Sampson, NY. He was assigned to USS *New York* at Norfolk, VA and participated in action in Iwo Jima and Okinawa.

Memorable experience: Jimmy Carter (future President) was a midshipman and part of the crew on one of their trips to Trinidad; also memorable was going through the Panama Canal, then to Long Beach, CA where Dinah Shore was singing to them from the docks.

In 1946 the *New York* served as a target ship in Operation Crossroads at the Bikini Atomic Tests. She was then decommissioned in August 1946, towed to Pearl Harbor and studied for two years. On July 8, 1948 she was towed out to sea and, after eight hours of pounding by ships and planes, was sunk.

Discharged April 15, 1946 and awarded APCM w/2 Battle Stars.

Employed by Holmes Protection Co. in New York City, he retired as manager in December 1995. Married to Mary K. since Oct. 29, 1971, he has two children, Denise and Karen, and one grandchild, Kristen.

JOHN T. OLIVER, Y2/c, born May 16, 1926 in Haddon Field, NJ. Enlisted in February 1944 at Philadelphia, PA. Attended boot camp at Camp Peary, VA; served on USS *Wyoming* and USS *New York*. Participated in Iwo Jima and Okinawa battles.

He never thought he would be a pointer on the 14-inch battery and be a helmsman midnight to 0400, steering a battleship. His father, John T. Oliver, CQM, USN also served on the USS *New York* in 1942.

Discharged in June 1946 and awarded American Defense, APCM w/2 stars, WWII Victory Medal and Combat Award Ribbon.

He became a registered architect in four states and had his own firm for 36 years. He is currently semi-retired as a construction inspector.

Married Gloria in 1979 and has three children: Dana Marie, Jamie Ann and Catherine Marie, and one grandchild, Allec.

ERNEST PATROLIA, born Jan. 6, 1924 in New Orleans, LA. Enlisted July 19, 1941. Attended boot camp at Norfolk, VA, then 16 weeks of Aviation Metalsmith School at Pensacola, FL. On graduation he was assigned to the USS *New York* (BB-34) and convoy duty to Iceland to relieve Marine Detachment.

Covered the North African Invasion from Casablanca to Safi. Stayed in ETO until surrender of German forces; went to Pacific and bombarded Iwo Jima; covered Okinawa invasion from start to finish. Flew in seaplanes as radio gunner and spotted ships fire. His pilot Lt. H. Nitz and himself rescued a downed pilot off the island where Ernie Pyle was killed. Flew 53 missions spotting ships fire over Iwo Jima and Okinawa. Stayed on *New York* until decommissioned. Transferred to Oceana NAS then to Milton, FL NAS.

Discharged Jan. 7, 1947 as AMM1/c and awarded DFC and six Air Medals. Enlisted in Active Reserve, made ADRC and retired at age 60. He has retired from NOPD and US Marshal Service and is doing whatever he feels like.

Married to Anna Jean Russell, he has four sons, two daughters, 11 grandchildren and three great-grandchildren.

RICHARD H.D. PIASECKI, SKC, born Sept. 2, 1918 in Philadelphia, PA. Enlisted in the Navy June 2, 1936 and received recruit training in Newport, RI. Shipped in transport *Chaumont* to West Coast and the fleet and assigned duty in the battleship *New York*.

In early 1937 he returned to East Coast. The *New York* was selected to represent the US in Portsmouth, England for the coronation of King George VI, May 12, 1937. There were many foreign warships present, including the Nazi Germany pocket battleship *Graf Spee*. The *New York* extended the honor of manning the rail for King George in the royal yacht as it passed in review of the foreign ships and the British home fleet.

He also took part in manning the rail honors on two occasions for President Franklin D. Roosevelt. Subsequent midshipmen summer training cruises followed with northern European ports of call. He was serving aboard gunboat *Erie* PG-50 out of Balboa, Panama, CZ, Dec. 7, 1941 when Pearl Harbor was attacked.

He attends annual New York reunions as often as possible. He last observed the *New York* at Bikini Atoll, M.I. as one of many target ships for Operation Crossroads Atomic Bomb Test Able and Baker in July 1946 while serving aboard Rockwall APA-230.

Married Margret O'Connor Dec. 24, 1940 in New York City and has two children, Carolyn and Guy; three grandchildren: Joyce, Jason and Nicholas.

GEORGE H. "ED" POMEROY, CAD, born April 30, 1921 in Bath, Maine. Graduated from Waltham High School, Waltham, MA. Entered the USN at Newport, RI, October 1940. Served on the USS *New York*, USS *Sangamon*, and USS *Kula Gulf*.

Participated in North Atlantic convoy, North African invasion, South Pacific and Solomons. Discharged December 1946

and awarded Atlantic Defense, APCM, EAME, Combat Action and Presidential Unit Citation. The entire six years was a memorable experience!

In civilian life he was a licensed FAA mechanic, licensed amateur radio operator and an insurance executive. Retired in 1983 as vice-president of Hamilton/Meridian Insurance. Enjoys ham radio, golf, family activities and is a three time cancer survivor.

Married JoAnn on Dec. 14, 1943 and has two children, Linda and Gary; three grandchildren: Troy, Scott and Layne.

ROBERT W. POWERS, Capt., USMC, born in Eatonton, GA Sept. 13, 1921. Enlisted May 6, 1941. Served on the USS *New York* from December 1942 to November 1944, then in a demonstrations company at Camp Lejeune; later instructor, Marine Corps Schools, Quantico, VA until discharged Feb. 14, 1946. Promoted to major in the USMCR.

Employed February 1946 to 1959 with Connecticut General Life Insurance (now CIGNA) in Lancaster, PA; Hartford, CT and St. Louis, MO. He built an insurance agency in Munich, Germany 1959-1960. Founded employee benefits and an actuarial consulting firm in St. Louis in 1960. In 1979 he sold the company which is now part of Buck Consultants, Inc. by whom he is still employed.

Married four times, has four children and enjoying life more each year.

The USS *New York* was a very fortunate, enlightening, if hairy, experience. It is now a pleasant recollection. Semper fi, you all.

NELSON B. PRICE, EM3/c, born Feb. 14, 1926. Inducted Aug. 3, 1944 in Richmond, VA and went aboard the *New York* in November 1944 as Seaman 2/c.

Left Norfolk, VA in 1944 for the West Coast. Stationed on No. 5 turret, 14-inch guns where his job was to pass the gun powder from the powder bin to the gun room. Stood watch on the 20mm anti-aircraft guns. Served aboard during the battles of Iwo Jima and Okinawa.

After the battle of Okinawa, he transferred to the electrical division and stood watch in the log room and maintained and serviced the telephone system.

Discharged April 30, 1946 and awarded American Area Campaign Medal, WWII Victory Medal and APCM w/2 stars. Obtained rank of EM3/c before leaving the ship in January 1946.

He retired as building and grounds superintendent at Piedmont Geriatric Hospital in 1988. Enjoys woodworking.

Married Anne Johnson on Dec. 24, 1951, they have three children: Leonard, Kimberly and Kelly; four grandchildren: Samuel, Anne and Peter Mills and Grant Hancock.

MARION "CARL" RAMBO, MM2/c, born Jan. 4, 1924 in Epthworth, SC and attended Greenwood, SC schools. Enlisted in USN Dec. 29, 1941. Attended recruit training at Norfolk, VA. Jan. 25, 1942 assigned duty on the USS *New York*.

The recorded history of the USS *New York* fully documents the many contributions to the war effort and he is proud to have served as a crew member. Transferred to the USS *Salisbury Sound* (AV-13) July 25, 1946 for duty at Okinawa. Due to an engine room accident he was sent to Alameda, CA, then on to USS *Bodoens Strait* CEV-116 Sept. 1, 1946 to assist in preparing the ship for sea duty.

Discharged March 14, 1937 and awarded Navy Arctic Service Ribbon, Navy E., Good Conduct Medal, American Area Campaign, EAME, APCM and WWII Victory Medal.

Retired as an engineering specialist after 34 years with DuPont. He enjoys woodworking, travel and reading.

Married Mary Emma Dukes Aug. 7, 1943 and has three children: Carl Jr., Carole and Janie.

HENRY R. "SHORTY" REYNOLDS, AA Gunner S2/c, USS *Wyoming* (BB-32), USS *New York* (BB-34), born Aug. 7, 1924 in Doddsville, MS. Inducted June 6, 1944 and was on the East Coast in early 1944, then through the Panama Canal. Joined the Iwo Jima assault in rehearsal at Saipan and went ahead of the main task force for the pre-invasion of Iwo Jima, February 16. Broke a propeller and went to Manus to a floating dry dock for repairs. In March went to the assault on Okinawa, where they spent a record time of 78 days. Left Okinawa June 11 to regun at Pearl Harbor; BB-34 was the first major ship to regun at a foreign port.

They were preparing for a trip to Japan when the war ended. In September 1945 they came back to California and were greeted by Dinah Shore. He was on the docking party and asked her on board for some good Navy coffee. They came to New York for Navy Day and at Christmas had orphans brought on board for Christmas dinner and gifts. This tradition was started aboard the USS *New York* in 1915.

He was discharged February 1946 from regular Navy, stayed in the USNR Stateside until December 1953. Awards include two Battles Stars and WWII Victory Medal.

The *New York* was offered to the state of New York and after refusal it was chosen to go to the A Bomb Test at Crossroads at Bikini, where she withstood the air burst and the underwater bomb. This was her last call to duty, her first call was Vera Cruz April 15, 1914.

After suffering five heart attacks and 22 years of hard work, he retired in 1979 as a warehouse and grain elevator manager and oil mill maintenance superintendent. He worked under O.J. "Slug" Jones of Texas, who was a chief petty officer on the USS *New York*. Since that time he has continued writing history of his area, state and the US Navy. He is a life member in the DAV, VFW, US Naval Institute and American Legion; he's also the coordinator of the USS *New York* reunions and their historian since WWII.

He married Odean on Aug. 26, 1944 and has four children: Henry Jr., Carrol Ann, Mickey and Joan; 13 grandchildren and 10 great-grandchildren.

MAURICE "GENE" ROBERTS, FC3/c, born Sept. 29, 1924 in Vinita, OK. Enlisted Sept. 2, 1942 at Tulsa, OK. Received basic training at San Diego, CA and attended Fire Control School at Newport, RI.

Assigned convoy duty to Casablanca from New York and participated in Iwo Jima and Okinawa invasions. For 1-1/2 years he was on the main and secondary gun directors; for 1-3/4 years he was gun director operator on quad 40mm mount 2, up forward, port side.

Discharged Dec. 22, 1945 and awarded North African Theater, APCM w/2 stars, American Defense and Good Conduct Medal. He re-enlisted in the USNR Oct. 3, 1948 and served until Nov. 9, 1952.

Attended San Anton Junior College and Trinity University on the GI Bill, received a BA degree. Retired after 18 years with Sears in Denver, CO and 15 years with Exxon, Fort Worth, TX. A life member of VFW, he is past quartermaster and commander, also belonged to the San Anton Jaycees and served as a scoutmaster. Enjoys camping, hunting and fishing.

Married to Nina Ruth June 9, 1948, she passed away Sept. 24, 1986 due to MS; remarried Stella May on Dec. 31, 1988. He has three children: Gene Jr., David Wayne and Nina Jean (married to Terry Perkins); three grandchildren: Dorenda, Steven, Selena (married to Tony Wilson) and one great-grandchild.

DOMINICK "ROCKIE" ROCCO, born in Morristown, NJ and attended elementary and high school there. Enlisted in USN in 1942 on the USS *New York* at Norfolk, VA on the Chesapeake Bay. On the ship he was a shoemaker and had his own shop. Participated at the battle of Iwo Jima and Okinawa.

Discharged February 1945 at Lido Bay, NY and awarded a Citation and two Battle Stars. His memory of being in the Navy was "Victory in the Pacific."

He had his own business for 43 years as a shoemaker in Madison, NJ. Enjoys gardening, golf and participating at the VFW, Post 3401.

Married to Virginia, he has three children and five grandchildren.

JOHN F. RYAN JR., RM3/c, born Sept. 2, 1925 in Providence, RI. Enlisted August 1943 in USN for "kiddie cruise." Attended boot camp at Sampson, NY; Radio School at Bainbridge, MD and boarded "Old Nick" in early 1944.

He made three midshipman cruises to Trinidad, then through the Panama Canal to participate in Iwo Jima invasion.

They returned to dry dock at Manus Island to repair broken prop and watched the Bob Hope show in dry dock. In March joined assault on Okinawa and spent record 78 days on firing line. They had returned to Pearl Harbor for gun repair when war ended.

Performed "Magic Carpet" duties returning GIs to the States and was part of Navy Day celebration in New York City. With a skeleton crew aboard, took BB-34 to Bikini for Operation Crossroads. Witnessed awesome power of two atomic bomb explosions. He was honorably discharged Nov. 15, 1945 at Brooklyn, NY.

Graduated from Providence College in 1951 on the GI Bill and retired from Merrill Lynch as vice-president in December 1990.

Married Barbara Healey in June 1949 and is the proud father of three children, 10 grandchildren and four great-grandchildren.

GENE SALLUZZO, born Dec. 7, 1925 in Hoosick Falls, NY. Entered active service Nov. 16, 1943 and received recruit training at Sampson, NY. Served in the USS *Mendocino*, USS *New York*, USS LCT (6), USS LST 133, USS *Latona* and at USNRS, Seattle, WA.

Memorable experience was going through the Panama Canal three times and seeing two A bomb tests. Discharged as coxswain and awarded APCM w/star, American Theater, Good Conduct Medal, Philippine Liberation and WWII Victory Medal.

He retired from the US Postal Service May 29, 1992 and enjoys volunteer work and walking.

Married to Mary L. Hewson (deceased) Dec. 27, 1952 and has three children: Susan, Toni and Jean Louis; 10 grandchildren: Corey, Brad, Evin, Christian, Jessica, Billy, Laura, Justin, Mary and Sara.

ROBERT F. "FRIENDLY" SMITH, born April 9, 1924 in Brooklyn, NY, son of career chief pharmacist mate. He grew up in San Diego, CA.

On active duty, July 1, 1943. Graduated from NROTC, University of Southern California in 1945. Served aboard USS *New York* in Secondary Battery Division, 1945-46; executive officer LCI (L) 546, 1946; COM 11 Public Information Office, 1946 and Reserve Public Relations Unit 11-1, 1947-55. Retired Sept. 5, 1961 and awarded American Theater, Pacific Theater w/star (Okinawa) and WWII Victory Medal.

Since 1964 he has served as president, chairman and chairman emeritus of Phillips-Ramsey Co., marketing and advertising agency in San Diego. Co-founder and chairman of Nuffer/Smith/Tucker, Inc., public relations, also headquarters in San Diego. Today he is president of Strategies & Teams, Inc., international consultants to companies, institutions and governments.

Married 1954 to Mary Rose Secan of Williams Lake, MI, and has four children: Cdr. Peter F. Smith USN, Matthew R. Smith (deceased), Mary Frances Smith-Reynolds and Barbara Anne Smith; two grandchildren, Mark P. Smith and Minna A. Smith.

KEN SPARKS, born Jan. 2, 1925 in Pittsburgh, PA. Enlisted Dec. 26, 1942 at Utica, NY and sworn in at Albany, NY Dec. 28, 1942. Attended boot camp Feb. 5, 1943 at Sampson NTS and Fire Control School, April 12, 1943 at NTS Newport, RI.

Assigned Oct. 15, 1943 to USS *New York* as FC3/c, 40mm director operator; training duty at Chesapeake Bay and midshipman cruises to Trinidad, summer 1944. In November 1944 he went through the Panama Canal and entered in battles at Iwo Jim and Okinawa; spent 76 days on line at Okinawa. They were getting new gun barrels at Pearl Harbor when war ended. Sailed from Pearl Harbor to New York City in 1944 with several hundred passengers aboard for discharge.

Discharged in January 1946 at Lido Beach, Long Island and entered Syracuse University in May 1946. Graduated in June 1949 and worked in sales, 1949-66 for four manufacturing companies. In October 1966 he purchased Wilcox Paper Co. in Syracuse and retired Jan. 2, 1990 leaving his sons to run the company.

Married Barbara on Dec. 28, 1946 and has four sons, Ralph, Warren, Dave and Brian; five grandsons, Doug, Jason, Erick, Andrew and Ben. They have attended all USS New York reunions and served as host and hostess at the 1994 reunion at Buffalo and the 1998 reunion at Cincinnati Airport in northern Kentucky.

CLIFTON RANDOLPH TERRELL, born Feb. 18, 1927 in Rocky Mount, NC, son of Rev. and Mrs. Irby D. Terrell. He was raised in Buena Vista, VA and graduated high school there. Sworn into the Navy before graduation and given a leave to finish high school. He spent his 18th birthday at Iwo Jima.

Upon leaving the service he went to Presbyterian Junior College, Maxton, NC for 12 months then entered Presbyterian College in Clinton, SC. Graduated in 1950 and entered Columbia Theological Seminary in Decatur, GA for three years.

His fields of service were Reidville and Antioch churches, Reidville, SC; Henry Belk Presbyterian Church, Anderson, SC; Old Laurel Hill Presbyterian Church, Laurinburg, NC; Stanley PC, Stanley, NC; Rutherford PC, Rutherford, NC; Crestwood PC, High Point, NC and Wildwood PC, Morehead City, NC. He retired in 1990 and moved to Hampstead, NC just 20 miles northeast of Wilmington, NC. Now lives five miles out of town and just half mile from the inland waterway. He keeps busy building birdhouses and keeping up his yard and garden.

CECIL THOMAS, served aboard the USS *New York* from June 1936 until return from Europe after the coronation cruise. He believes it was sometime in August 1937. He was then transferred to a four-stacker, the *Williamson*, 244.

He recalls Stegmire, sailor and good friend, who fell to his death from a window in the Bronx in June 1940.

EDWARD N. TOMPKINS, RDM1/c, born Oct. 10, 1922 in Lincoln, IL. Enlisted in USN March 3, 1943 at Lincoln, IL. Boarded the USS *New York* in June 1943 at Casco Bay, ME and participated in Iwo Jima and Okinawa battles.

He was discharged in June 1948 from the Navy and enlisted in the Air Force the same month. Most of his medals are from the Air Force.

Retired from Hamilton AFB, CA July 1967 and enjoys golfing, fishing and yard work.

Married Doris Margaret May 23, 1942 and has six children: Sandra, Michael, Mark, Bruce, Anna Marie and Matthew; 10 grandchildren: Gina, Paul, Jeff, Erin, Todd, Conor, Parker, Nicholas, Courtney and Sutton.

ROBERT "BOB" URBAN, RDM2/c, volunteered for the Navy March 2, 1943 and assigned to the USS *New York* May 19, 1943 to April 7, 1944. After 10 months he was transferred to the destroyer USS *Mayrant* 402. They did convoy duty to Europe and Africa.

After the war was over in Europe they went through the Panama Canal on their way to Japan. In their stop at Hawaii, he was sent to a Radar Maintenance School and during that time the war ended.

His memorable experience was when he was a mess cook and had to get five 5 pound bags of coffee beans from below the main deck and his buddy knocked one of the bags off his shoulder, splitting it open. When Bob chased him to help pick them up, he dove at his back and hit an iron overhead beam and had to have five stitches.

Retired from Union Carbide Co. in Ottawa, IL in 1986. Enjoys model airplanes, cooking and following the Chicago Cubs.

He married Jeannette Stirratt June 19, 1948 and has two children, Judith Bosshart and Dianne Derango; seven grandchildren: Megan, Stephen and Brie Bosshart and John, Lucas, Jenna and Christina Derango.

LEO WALTHERS, Aviation Ordnanceman 2/c, born Jan. 19, 1921 in New York, NY. Enlisted Nov. 14, 1940 and attended recruit training at Newport, RI. On Jan. 5, 1941 he reported aboard the USS *New York* as an apprentice seaman assigned to Division IV.

Later transferred to the aviation unit as an aviation ordnanceman, which serviced three Kingfisher (OS2U) observation planes. In June 1942 he was detached and transferred to the Naval Air Technical Training Center as an aviation chief ordnance instructor.

Retired after 22 years of naval service and presently resides in Warner Robins, GA.

Hospital Division, USS New York, Pacific Ocean Area, 1945.

The FM Division, 1944.

USS *NEW YORK* SHIPMATES "TAPS" 1970-2001

Submitted by H.R. Shorty Reynolds

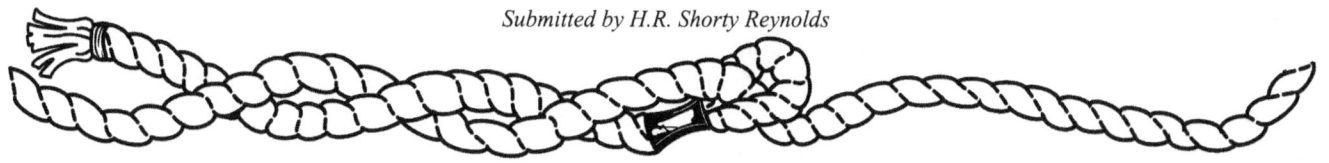

Adams, Sam E.
Adkins, Ora
Allison, R.C.
Almgreen, H.E.
Anderson, Fred
Andonach, R.E.
Armstrong, W.L.
Bankston, L.J.
Barnard, F.B.
Barnes, John
Becker, W.E.
Beloat, Wes
Benton, Drexel
Beverly, Merle D.
Bloomingdale, Lyman (Bill)
Bone, Everitt
Branca, Mike
Brewer, Jim
Britt, O'neal
Brock, Garth
Brooks, Howard
Brown, James
Buck, Hugh
Burley, E.G.
Busch, Harry E.
Carter, A.
Carter, Phil
Cash, W.J.
Cassidy, Rex
Chamberlain, R.D.
Champeau, Harold
Chase, John
Christensen, Bob
Clark, Ken?
Clark, Lester
Cobb, Herbert G.

Cole, James A.
Copeland, Bill
Cora, Jesse
Cothran, C.L.
Countryman, Eddie
Covey, Donald
Custlow, George
Dalton, Claude A.
Davis, Sam
Dawson T.J.
Davis, Vic R.
Dedig, G.P. (Bud)
Delong, C.L.
Dennis, James
Dessert, Eugene
Dew, Richard (Botz)
Dietz, Frank
Dodd, James
Downing, Oliver
Doyle, William H.
Dreilling, Ken
Duke, Perry E.
Dunn, W.C.
Durbin, Charles
Edwards, Lowell
Elliot, James
Ellis, John
Ellyson, Cliff
Ethridge, Ed
Ethridge, Harrison
Farris, Walter
Feathers, Charles
Felt, David
Fisk, Clarence
Fletcher, Howard
Flicking, G.W.

Fraser, F.C. (Pappy)
Frey, Walter
Fries, Fred (Bald Eagle)
Fry, Hubert
Fuller, W.H.
Gardner, Eugene
Gardner, Hezie
Garrison, (Big) Jim
Gerr, Clifton
Gilder, Van
Gire, Howard
Gould, Ralph
Graft, Art
Green, Herb
Griffin, Ellis
Grinstead, Ed
Gross, Elmer
Grote, ?____
Grubbs, Joseph
Guerrier, Frank
Hahne, Charles
Hall, Rex
Halstrom?, A.L.?
Hamlin, W.P.
Hanna, N.
Hardsety, C.
Harless, Herbert
Harris, R. L.
Harris, Wilson
Harthshorne, Dallas
Haskew, Hop
Henderson, Jim
Hercheck, Sammy
Herrick, John J.
Hestbeck, Elmer
Hickman, Walter

93

Hicks, Darl
Higgins, Charles
Hill, Roy
Hinz, Rudolph
Hogland, Harrison
Holley, William S.
Holmes, Charles
Hopper, Arvil ??
Houck, Merle
Howard, Sherman
Howell, George
Howell, J.E.
Howman, Richard
Hubner, Merle
Huey, James
Hughes, Steven
Jackin, Charles
Johansen, Theodore
Johanssen, Earl
Jones, Sidney
Jurgenson, M.C.
Kane, James B.
Keeton, Gary
Keller, W.K.
Kelly, John
Kemper, Marvin
Kersey, J.R.
Ketnor, Roy
Keublin, D.W.
Kinnan, ?____
Kinnedy, Basil
Klaus, Gregory
Klweberg?, Al
Knox, James
Kolbe, Arthur
Krouse, R.J.
Lagaey, Virgil (Leggs)
Lewis, W.B.
Lilley, James
Lincoln, Author
Lockwood, Harris
Lomker, ?____
Lorentz, Tom
Macones, L.E.
Manning, Roy
Marker, Carl
Marks, Paul
Martin, Joe
Matheussen, J.L.
Mathissen, Walter
Matison, Robert

May, Tom
McCone, William
McKennan, K.K.
McKnight, Francis
McLenski, John
McMillen, John
McWilliams, Cecil
Meredith, Paul
Metz, Alfred
Metz, Roger
Millard, Jack
Miller, John
Mishue, Philip
Mittchell, William
Mooney, John
Morris, Cecil
Morrison, T.L.
Mullens, Moon
Murphy, Dennis
Muse, H.C. (D Lo)
Newberry, J.M.
Nitz, Bill
O'Brian, Robert
Odom, Earl
Ownsby, Charles
Papas, Robert
Parkin, Walter
Parks, Floyd
Paske, J.H.
Pederson, John
Perks, Raymon
Phelps, Gordon
Pittman, Joseph
Poppler, Elliott
Pratt, M.R.
Preston, Carlos
Price, C.J.
Randolph, Charles
Restop?, Stanton
Reynolds, Merle
Riley, Joseph
Ritter, L.P.
Robinson, Leonard
Rosenberg, Charles
Ross, Mel
Russell, Robert
Ryman, R.L.
Scott, Matthew
Scully, Joseph A.
Sharkey, W. (Lucky)
Shaum, Ray

Shell?, Earl
Shelton, J.D.
Shrader, Clarence
Sikes, Richard
Small, Alex
Smith, Granville
Smith, Marion
Snow, Francis J.
Sparrow, Harry
Spears, Gerald
Spellman, Edward
Standars, J.L.
Stewart, Howard C.
Stone, J.L.
Stubbs, Paul
Sudberry, Ellis
Sullivan, Howard
Sullivan, Paul
Swan, Eugene
Sweet, Herbert,
Swetzer, Bob
Taylor, Monroe
Teach, John
Thompson, Joseph
Thornburg, Max
Tierce, M.B.
Tinchler, Lex
Trumbell, M.A.
Trysen, William
Tucker, Ferrell
Turner, Joseph
Twilly, Carrol
Tynes, Claude
Urbaetis, W. Joseph
Veeh, W.G.
Warden, Robert
Wellock, Dan
Wenger, Claude
West, Robert
Wheeler, ?___
Wheeler, T.H.
Wilkins, Glene
Williams, Paul (Dead Pan)
Willis, Hoyt
Wilson, John
Wiseman, Glenn
Wisnkder, Ed
Wolf, Charles
Wright, Robert
Wymer, Charles
Yellig, R.J.

INDEX

A

Admiralty Islands 61, 69, 71
Akron 43
Albert, BB Jr. 70
Aleutian Islands 18
Alphonse Delanade 35
America 7, 13, 14, 23, 24, 25
Annapolis 37, 44
Anzio 23
Argonaut 71
Armstrong, William 8
Asia 25
Attu Islands 18
Augusta 36
Australia 17

B

Bal, Charles 54
Balboa 73, 74
Bantry Bay 14
Belgium 46
Benbow 73
Bernadou 35
Berrigan, John 54
Betio Island 18
Beverly Hills 59
Bibby, Capt. L.H. 55
Bibby, CPO 64
Bier, PFC 59
Bikini Atoll 24, 38, 46, 55, 56
Birmingham 76
Bismarch 53
Bismarck Sea 71
Bismark 16
Black Prince 71
Blakiston, T.V. 59
Bloomfield 76
Boston 43, 66, 67, 75
Boxer 57
Brainard, Harry 63
Brinkman, PFC 59
Britain 15
British Isles 42
Brophy, Harry 77
Buckner Bay 54
Burton 54
Byrne, J.J. 57

C

Calder, Elsie 31
California, State of 37, 55, 58, 75
Cape Blanco 74
Caribbean 13, 32, 53
Caribbean Sea 40
Carter, Capt. Grayson B. 53, 58, 63, 65, 74
Carter, Phillip R. 42
Casablanca 23, 34, 36, 40, 43, 53
Casco Bay 43, 66

Champeau, Harold C. 70
Cherbourg 23
Chesapeake 53
Chesapeake Bay 40, 77
Chevelier, PFC 59
China 7, 17, 24, 62, 69
Christian, Captain K.C. 54, 59, 60, 71
Clamp 47
Cleveland, City of 56
Clipperton Island 74
Coden 44
Cole 35
Connaught, Prince of 58
Connecticut 10
Connell, Lt Cmdr 74
Connor, Daniel 57
Coral Sea 17, 64
Corbesier 71
Costa Rica 73
Crescent City 73
Cristobal 60
Cuba 14, 64
Cummins, Chaplain 43

D

Davidson, Lyle 35
Davis, Captain Guy 55
Del Orleans 73
Delaware 10
Dixie 73

E

Edinburgh 42
Emerson, Arnold C. 59
England 12, 13, 14, 23, 33, 57, 66
Eniwetok 18, 44, 60
Enterprise 17, 18
Europe 9, 13, 16, 23, 24, 25, 67

F

Fall River 24
Fedala 36, 43
Fletcher, Frank 31
Florida 10, 32
Formosa 61
Fort de France 77
France 13, 32
Fraser, Admiral 71
Fraser, Sir Bruce 71
Frisco Islands 44
Fuller, J.E.C. 12
Fulton, Robert 7

G

Gambier Bay 22
Georgia, State of 67
Germany 12, 15, 27, 31, 42, 56

Gilbert Islands 17, 18
Glasgow 65
Great Britain 27, 31
Greenwich 77
Greer, Marshall R. 56
Grennock 42, 65
Guadalcanal 17, 18, 35
Guam 21
Guantanamo Bay 64
Guderian, Heinz 12
Gulfport 46

H

H. M. Hood 16
Hall 54
Halsey, Admiral 21, 22
Hampton Roads 33, 52
Hansen, Commander 73
Hart, B.H. Liddel 12
Hatfield 67
Havana 14
Hawaii 44, 46, 54, 59, 63, 75
Hei 18
Hill, Vice Admiral 45
Hirohito, Admiral Prince 46, 58
Hirohito, Emperor 31, 58
Hiroshima 23
Hitler 67
HMS Avenger 71
HMS Benbow 73
HMS Black Prince 71
HMS Dreadnought 29
HMS George V 71
HMS Invincible 71
HMS Reaper 71, 73
Hodgekiss, PFCs 59
Hoke, Nelson G. 59
Honolulu 57
Hood 54
Hoosick Falls 77
Hoover 15
Hornet 18
Howe 71
Huerta 31
Hughes, James Ryan 57
Hugues, John F. 57
Hungnam Harbor 24
Husdale, Cprl 78

I

Iceland 23, 34, 35, 40, 42, 53, 65, 66
Ie Shima 45, 54
Illinois 10
Inchon 24
Indian Ocean 73
Ireland 14
Island of Martinique 77
Italy 13, 15, 23
Iwo Jima 17, 21, 22, 37, 38, 40, 44, 53, 55, 56, 57, 60, 61, 63, 64, 68, 69, 70, 73, 75, 77

J

Japan 7, 14, 15, 17, 21, 22, 29, 31, 37, 38, 42, 44, 45, 46, 55, 58, 61, 63, 66, 74, 77
Jean Bart 23, 36, 43
Jean-Baptiste LeMoyne 74
Johnson, Admiral 55
Johnston 22
Jutland 12, 31

K

Kazan Retto 69
Kearny 34
Kearsarge 10
Keller, Lt. 63
Kerama Rhetto 45, 54, 61
Kess, Christine 77
Kiel 56
King George V 31
King George VI 34, 57
Kinkaid, Vice Admiral 21
Kirishima 18
Kiska Islands 18
Korea 11, 25
Kwajalein 18, 50, 55
Kyushu 37

L

Lagaly, Lt. Virgil "Legs" 76
Laws 54
Leary 34
Lebanon 11, 25
LeMoyne 74
Leutze 71, 73
Leyte 21, 22, 45, 63
Lieberman, Chief 71
Lilley, James 44
Long Beach 44, 60
Los Angeles 58
Los Negros 71
Louisville 54
Luzon 21, 22

M

MacArthur, Gen. Douglas 17, 55
Mahan, Alfred Thayer 13
Makin Island 18
Mannion 60
Manus 37, 44, 45, 59, 61, 69, 70, 71, 72, 73
Mariana Islands 17, 18, 60
Marseilles 23
Marshall Islands 17, 18, 19, 60, 77
McCoy 67
McCrea, J.L. 57

95

Mediterranean 6, 25
Meridith, 2nd Lt. Paul 76
Mexico 53
Middle East 7
Midway Islands 17
Mobile 24, 54
Morin, Eugene 57
Morocco 43, 46, 53
Murmansk 23

N

Nagagusuku Wan 72
Nagasaki 23
New Guinea 17, 71
New Orleans 42, 46, 54, 73, 74
New York - City, State of 19, 23, 31, 42, 43, 46, 54, 55, 57, 58, 59, 60, 65, 68, 73, 76
Newfoundland 42, 65
Newport 63
Nicaragua 74
Nimitz, Admiral 17
Nippon 56
Norfolk 16, 29, 32, 33, 35, 42, 43, 44, 48, 64, 66, 68
Normandy 23, 77
North Africa 23, 34, 35, 40, 53, 67
North Korea 24
Norway 24
Nova Scotia 42, 43, 65

O

O'Casey, Sean 72
Okinawa 17, 21, 23, 37, 40, 43, 45, 47, 51, 53, 54, 56, 57, 58, 60, 61, 62, 63, 68, 72, 75, 76, 77
Oldendorf, Rear Admiral 22

P

Paixhans, Henri 8
Panama 44, 46, 54, 59, 60, 68, 73, 74, 77
Pawtucket 57
Pearl Harbor 11, 12, 16, 17, 19, 24, 25, 28, 35, 38, 44, 45, 46, 50, 54, 55, 56, 58, 59, 60, 62, 63, 66, 68, 73, 76
Persian Gulf 25
Peyton, Lt 78
Philadelphia 35, 36, 45
Philippine Sea 21
Philippines 17, 21, 45, 59, 63, 77
Point De La Tour 35
Pomeroy, George 19, 63, 74
Port-Of-Spain 73
Portland 43, 66
Portsmouth 42, 57
Powers, Lt 78
Price, Henry 67
Price, Nelson B. 67
Prince of Wales 16, 31
Puerto Rico 64

Puget Sound 16
Pyle, Ernest 45, 54

R

Railleuse 43
Rankin, Lt. Cmdr. Dan 57, 69
Reclaimer 46, 47, 49, 50
Repulse 16
Ressel, Joseph 8
Reuben James 34
Reykjavik 65
Reynolds, H. R. 39, 50, 53, 56, 78
Rhode Island 66
Richelieu 23
Roberts, "Chuck" 63
Rocco, Dominick 77
Rockbridge 46, 47, 48
Rodgers, Thomas S. 31
Rodman, Admiral Hugh 31, 33, 53, 58
Rome 6
Rooks 54
Roosevelt, Franklin D. 10, 24, 33, 45, 54, 66
Roosevelt, Lt. Col James 55
Rosythe 57
Russia 13, 23
Ryukyus 45

S

S.S. Mercy 66
Safi 35, 40, 43, 53
Saipan 21, 44, 60
Salerno 23
Salluzzo, Eugene 77
Salluzzo, Gene 54
San Bernadino 22
San Diego 63
San Francisco 19, 25
San Jacinto 24
San Jose 74
San Pedro 38, 45, 46, 54, 58
Santee 36
Santiago 14
Saratoga 17, 18
Savo Island 17, 18
Scapa Flow 31
Scotland 31, 35, 40, 42, 43, 53, 65, 66
Seattle 77
Seeadler Bay 71
Shore, Dinah 38, 58
Shuri Castle 53
Sicily 23
Smith, Admiral Allen E. 60
Smith, Ensign Bob "Friendly" 76
Solomon Islands 17
South America 14
South Carolina 10
South Dakota 18
Spain 14, 16
Spellman, Francis J. 57, 60
SS North Carolina 23

St. Louis 34, 54
Strub, Denise 55
Suisun Bay 25
Surigao Strait 22
Syria 25

T

Taranto 28
Tarawa Atoll 18, 53
Teheran 24
Tennessee, State of 67
Terrell, Randolph 75
Thompson, Lt. Joseph S. 69, 75
Thompson, Marie A. 69
Tinian Islands 21
Tirpitz 24
Tokyo 54, 61, 62
Trinidad 37, 44, 59, 77
Tropic of Cancer 72
Truk Islands 18
Truman, Harry 54
Tuscaloosa 44

U

Ulithi 44, 45, 73, 61
United States 7, 11, 12, 13, 14, 15, 16, 17, 23, 24, 25, 53, 56, 58
USS Alabama 17, 21, 23, 24, 53
USS Arizona 12, 16, 24, 25, 37
USS Arkansas 16, 23, 24, 28, 29, 34, 37, 53, 55, 60
USS Brooklyn 34, 36, 42, 52, 57, 68
USS California 13, 16, 20, 21, 22, 24, 25
USS Cassin 71, 73
USS Clamp 47
USS Colorado 15, 16, 18, 21, 22, 37, 53
USS Conklin 71
USS Consolation 69
USS Constitution 64
USS Crescent City 73
USS Delaware 14
USS Deliver 47
USS Enterprise 17
USS Florida 14
USS Franklin 7
USS Hope 69
USS Idaho 16, 18, 21, 23, 37, 53, 60
USS Independence 7
USS Indiana 8, 9, 10, 13, 14, 15, 17, 18, 20, 21, 23, 24
USS Ingram 42
USS Iowa 8, 10, 13, 14, 15, 17, 20, 21, 22, 23, 24, 25, 30
USS Maine 10, 13, 14
USS Maryland 13, 16, 17, 18, 21, 22, 23, 24, 37, 53, 62
USS Massachusetts 8, 13, 14, 15, 17, 21, 22, 23, 24, 36, 53
USS Mississippi 16, 17, 18, 21, 22, 24, 53

USS Missouri 8, 17, 23, 24, 25, 45, 53, 63
USS Montana 15
USS Nevada 10, 13, 14, 15, 16, 18, 23, 24, 28, 29, 37, 53, 59, 62
USS New Hampshire 14
USS New Jersey 8, 9, 10, 11, 17, 21, 22, 23, 24, 25
USS New Mexico 16, 18, 21, 22, 23, 28, 53, 54
USS New York 25, 53, 55
USS North Carolina 10, 15, 16, 17, 18, 21, 24, 53
USS Oklahoma 12, 14, 16, 24, 29, 37
USS Oregon 8, 13, 14
USS Pennsylvania 13, 14, 16, 18, 21, 22, 24, 53
USS Preserver 48
USS Quincey 64
USS Reclaimer 46
USS Rockbridge 46
USS Sangamon 66
USS South Dakota 15, 17, 18, 21, 24
USS Tennessee 13, 16, 18, 21, 23, 24, 37, 53, 62
USS Texas 13, 14, 16, 23, 24, 27, 29, 32, 33, 34, 37, 53, 62
USS Utah 14, 32
USS Vincennes 64
USS Washington 7, 16, 18, 21
USS West Virginia 13, 16, 21, 24, 53, 54
USS Widgeon 50
USS Wisconsin 8, 17, 21, 24, 25
USS Wyoming 10, 14, 16, 28, 29, 32, 37, 53

V

Vera Cruz 31, 53
Versailles 32
Vietnam 11, 25
Virginia 10, 33

W

Waltham 63
Washington 18, 23
Wasp 17, 18
Watt, James 7
Wellock, Daniel 43
West Indies 37
West Virginia 22, 23, 34, 37, 62
Widgeon 50
Wilson, President 32
Wilson, Woodrow 31

Y

Yamamoto 8
Yokosuka 74
Young 71, 73

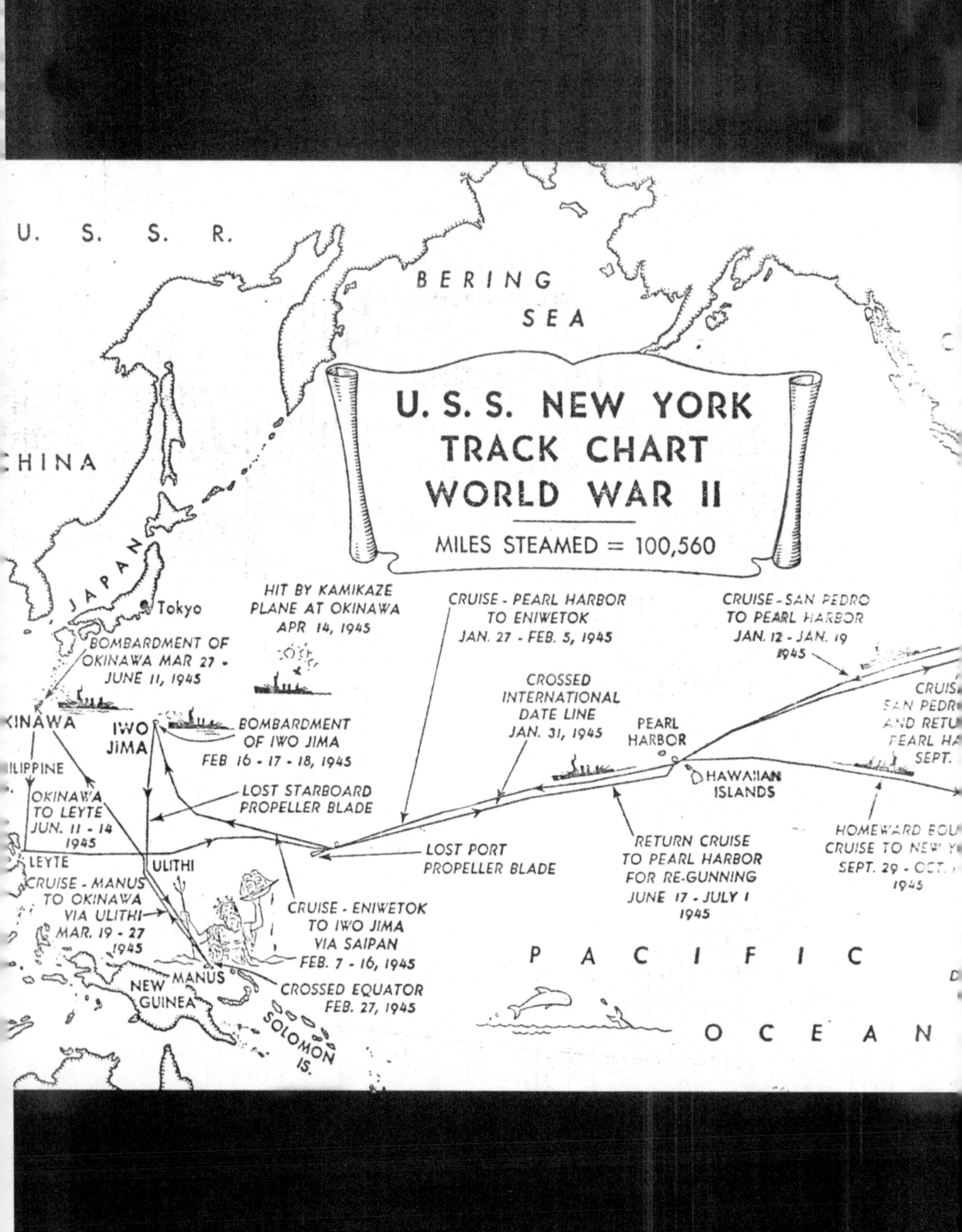

www.ingramcontent.com/pod-product-compliance
Lightning Source LLC
Chambersburg PA
CBHW082142230426
43672CB00016B/2938